Trump Madness

That Really Happened?!

Brad McCormick

A Modernizing Comprehensive Learning for All Production
November 2023

ISBN: 9798868272578

www.mclearningforall.com

For Everyone
Who Thought:
"Hold up. No way!"

Table of Contents

Trump Madness

The four years of the Trump Presidency was filled with so much Madness you may have missed just how Mad it was. Jump into a Game of "Trump Madness: That Actually Happened?!" to see if you, your family, your friends, or anyone you're trying to convince that another Donald Trump Presidency is a bad idea can correctly identify events that actually happened during the Trump Presidency. There are 100 events contained within these pages, but which are Real and which are Fake? Hint: A lot of them are Real.

The Real events must be verifiable with sources, otherwise it is just another Mad story which may or may not be Real. Additionally, they must have occurred during the Trump Presidency between 1/20/2017 and 1/19/2021. The events included are not exhaustive of his Presidency. There is a lot more Madness out there.

The four years of the Trump Presidency were truly unprecedented. Maybe we could all use a refresher on just how Mad things got on a regular basis. Good luck. Take breaks as needed.

WARNING

This is not just for fun. The Real events provide a sobering retrospective on the events of the Trump Presidency. Real people were hurt, on a regular basis, because one man who only cares about himself ascended to the Presidency of the United States of America. We cannot let it happen again. We'll get lost in the Madness.

Code: Event Title

If the Event is either Real or Fake

Date of Event and QR Code to Source

If the QR doesn't work, check out the Short URLs on page 122.

Madness Rating: 0 - 10 MAGA Hats

0 = Not Mad  **10 = Maddest**

*****Available in .25 (¼) Increments*****

The Ranking Rules

The entire idea for putting together Trump's Presidential Madness in a book like this came from my interactions on an internet message board. As we were approaching the 2024 election posters started to bring up some of the past Mad events of the Trump Presidency. Some people were questions if some of the events were real and others were attempting to figure out which event was the Maddest.

It was at that time I offered to run a March Madness Style Tournament.* I used a Google Sheet to Collect all possible entrants and grouped them by the "regions" used in this book, Google Drawings to create a 64 event Trump Madness Bracket, and Google Forms for Seeding our 100+ entries and then to conduct the voting in each round.

During our month long tournament we had many debates about what the criteria for being "Mad" was. Stupidity? Insanity? Awful? Harmful? Spiteful? Hypocritical? Each poster had their own unique priority order which led to many match ups being decided by 1 vote, including the finals. The Madness rankings here mostly follow our bracket, but I personally favor Stupidity, Harmful, and Hypocritical, so those have a heavy influence in the final Madness rankings.

***Full Bracket Results Located on Pages 129 - 133**

How to Play

1 Scan the QR Code

2 Spin the Wheel

3 Go to the Directory to Find the Event You Spun

4 Guess if the Event was

5 Go to the Page to See if You Are Correct!

The Directory

Things Trump Did

Starts On Page:

Contains actions that Trump actually took while President of the United States.

Things Trump Said

Starts On Page:

Contains things Trump actually said while President of the United States.

Trump Around the World

Starts On Page:

Contains things Trump actually did on the World Stage while President of the United States.

Trump World

Starts On Page:

Contains things people who were connected to the Trump Presidency actually did.

Things Trump Did

Things Trump Did

Code	Event	Page #
TD 9	Trump Visits Puerto Rican Hurricane Victims, Throws Them Paper Towels **Date:** 10/3/2017	42
TD 10	In the First of Many Times, Trump has a Problem Drinking Water **Date:** 11/15/2017	44
TD 11	Fires Andrew McCabe Two Days Before His Pension Kicks In **Date:** 3/16/2018	51
TD 12	First Reports of Donald Trump Regularly Ripping Up Documents **Date:** 6/10/2018	55
TD 13	Trump Meets with Putin and Takes his Translator's Notes **Date:** 7/16/2018	60
TD 14	Trump Proclaims National Golf Day, Also Happens to be Obama's B-Day **Date:** 8/4/2018	62
TD 15	Trump Does Event with Farmers on a Farm, Just Watches them Work **Date:** 9/2/2018	63
TD 16	In Just One Example of Many, Trump Tells a Story about Big Crying Men **Date:** 9/7/2018	64

Things Trump Did

Code	Event	Page #
TD 17	Trump has a Meeting with Kanye West in the Oval Office **Date:** 10/11/2018	**69**
TD 18	Appoints a Deputy AG Who Once Made Large Penis Toilets **Date:** 11/7/2018	**70**
TD 19	Serves Fast Food Buffet to the National College Football Champions **Date:** 1/14/2019	**75**
TD 20	Trump Gives a Speech, Demands the USS McCain Destroy be Moved **Date:** 5/28/2019	**80**
TD 21	Trump Uses a Marker to Draw an Extra Hurricane Path to be Right **Date:** 9/4/2019	**87**
TD 22	Moves Black Lives Matter Protesters for Photo Op w/ Upside Down Bible **Date:** 6/1/2020	**95**
TD 23	Trump isn't Just Afraid of Stairs, He Also Has Problems with Ramps **Date:** 6/13/2020	**96**
TD 24	Chris Christie Helps Trump w/ Debate Prep, Trump Gives him COVID **Date:** 9/26/2020	**105**

Things Trump Did

Code	Event	Page #
TD 25	Trump Lies, Goes to Presidential Debate While he has COVID **Date:** 9/29/2020	**107**
TD 26	While in the Hospital with COVID, Trump "Works", Signs Blank Papers **Date:** 10/3/2020	**108**
TD 27	While He has COVID, Trump Makes Secret Service Take Him for a Ride **Date:** 10/5/2020	**109**
TD 28	After COVID, Trump Returns to the White House, Has Issues Breathing **Date:** 10/5/2020	**110**
TD 29	Trump Finally Unveils His Healthcare Plan, A Giant Binder with Blank Paper **Date:** 10/21/2020	**112**
TD 30	In a Last Ditch Effort to Stay in Power, Trump Attempts a Literal Coup **Date:** 1/6/2021	**116**

Things Trump Said

Things Trump Said

Code	Event	Page #
TS 9	One of Many Incidents where Trump Thinks You Need an ID to Buy Food **Date:** 7/31/2018	**61**
TS 10	Describing a Hurricane: "The Wettest from the Standpoint of Water." **Date:** 9/18/2018	**65**
TS 11	Trump Tells Reporters He is Working on Making the White House Taller **Date:** 10/7/2018	**68**
TS 12	Trump Tells People Wounded Veterans are Cowards and Losers **Date:** 11/10/2018	**71**
TS 13	Trump Asks a 7 Year Old if He Still Believes in Santa, Which is Recorded **Date:** 12/24/2018	**74**
TS 14	Trump Calls Apple CEO Tim Cook "Tim Apple", He Had a Name Plate **Date:** 3/6/2019	**76**
TS 15	In an Ongoing Battle with Windmills, Trump Claims they Cause Cancer **Date:** 4/2/2019	**79**
TS 16	While Tweeting About NASA, Trump Claims the Moon is a Part of Mars **Date:** 6/7/2019	**81**

Things Trump Said

Things Trump Said

Trump Around the World

Code	Event	Page #
TAW 1	Trump Leaks Israeli Intelligence to Russians in White House Meeting **Date:** 5/10/2017	**29**
TAW 2	On a Trip in the Middle East, Trump Poses for a Photo Touching an Orb **Date:** 5/21/2017	**32**
TAW 3	Trump Meets the Pope and the Pictures from the Event are Very Odd **Date:** 5/24/2017	**33**
TAW 4	Trump Pushes a World Leader to Ensure a Spot in the Front of a Photo **Date:** 5/25/2017	**34**
TAW 5	Trump Discusses Local Milk People w/ the Australian Prime Minister **Date:** 8/3/2017	**39**
TAW 6	Trump Feeds Fish in Japan by Dumping All the Food Out **Date:** 11/6/2017	**43**
TAW 7	Trump Uses Twitter to Tell North Korea He Will Nuke Them **Date:** 1/2/2018	**46**
TAW 8	The TRUMP Brand Signs Removed from International Properties **Date:** 3/5/2018	**50**

Trump Around the World

Code	Event	Page #
TW 9	Trump Brings McDonalds to the G7 Summit in Canada **Date:** 6/7/2018	**53**
TAW 10	Trump is Photographed being Scolded by Other World Leaders **Date:** 6/9/2018	**54**
TAW 11	On a Visit to Meet Up with Kim Jong Un, Trump Salutes North Koreans **Date:** 6/14/2018	**56**
TAW 12	Trump Walks Directly in Front of the Queen of England and Just Stays **Date:** 7/13/2018	**57**
TAW 13	Makes Secret Service Stay at His International Property, They Pay Him **Date:** 7/14/2018	**58**
TAW 14	During a Live Press Conference, Trump Cowers to Putin **Date:** 7/16/2018	**59**
TAW 15	World Leaders Laugh at Trump During His United Nations Speech **Date:** 9/25/2018	**66**
TAW 16	Trump Said He and Kim Jong Un are in Love, Write Letters to Each Other **Date:** 9/29/2018	**67**

Trump Around the World

Trump World

Code	Event	Page #
TW 1	Sean Spicer Starts His New Job by Lying About Trump's Crowd Size **Date:** 1/21/2017	18
TW 2	Kellyanne Conway Says They Don't Lie, They Have Alternative Facts **Date:** 1/22/2017	19
TW 3	Trump's Personal Security Gets into a Fight with the Secret Service **Date:** 1/23/2017	20
TW 4	Trump Appoints Eric's Wedding Planner to a Position at the HUD **Date:** 6/16/2017	36
TW 5	Trump Hires Scaramucci to Head Communications, He Lasts 11 Days **Date:** 7/21/2017	37
TW 6	Michael Wolff Book Released, Wrote by Hanging Out at White House **Date:** 1/5/2018	47
TW 7	The Official Presidential Doctor Says Trump is Amazingly Healthy **Date:** 1/16/2018	48
TW 8	Trump Aide Sam Nunberg Goes on Multiple TV News Shows Drunk **Date:** 3/5/2018	49

Trump World

Code	Event	Page #
TW 9	Trump's Personal Lawyer Admits in Court Sean Hannity is Also a Client **Date:** 4/16/2018	**52**
TW 10	Melania Trump Does the Christmas Decorations and they are Creepy **Date:** 11/26/2018	**73**
TW 11	Turns Out Jared Kushner Couldn't Get A Security Clearance, Overruled **Date:** 4/1/2019	**78**
TW 12	Ivanka Trump Attends a World Leader Events and Gets Ignored by Everyone **Date:** 6/29/2019	**82**
TW 13	Trump's Personal Doctor Tells Him Eating Vegetables Gives You COVID **Date:** 3/13/2020	**91**
TW 14	Herman Cain Attends a Trump Rally, Dies of COVID a Month Later **Date:** 6/20/2020	**97**
TW 15	The Trumps Replace the Rose Garden with a Bunch of Bushes **Date:** 7/27/2020	**100**
TW 16	Trump's MAGA Base Creates Boaters for Trump, 5 Boats Sink **Date:** 9/5/2020	**104**

Trump World

Code	Event	Page #
TW 17	During Vice Presidential Debate a Fly Lands and Stays on Pence's Head **Date:** 10/7/2020	**111**
TW 18	Rudy Giuliani Has Press Conference at Four Seasons Total Landscaping **Date:** 11/7/2020	**113**
TW 19	While Defending Trump's Election Fraud Claims, Rudy's Hair Dye Melts **Date:** 11/19/2020	**114**

TS1: CIA Crowd Size

Date: 1/21/2017

Source:

The very first full day of the Trump Presidency, Donald Trump Visited the CIA. While standing in front of the CIA Memorial Wall, a wall with 140 stars representing the 140 members of the CIA who lost their lives in service to the United States of America, Trump gave a speech where he railed against the Media for failing to properly cover his crowd size at his Inauguration. Contrary to all evidence, Donald Trump claims he has the largest crowd for an Inauguration, ever. The crowd, he says, is huge and the Media refuses to cover that information correctly because they hate him, of course.

As horrible as this imaginary slight might be, he might have gotten more sympathy if he, a draft dodger who never served the United States of America in his life, didn't complain about it directly in front a memorial for those who sacrificed everything for it. Starting off his reign strong and giving us a great look at what we had to look forward to.

TW1: Sean Spicer

Date: **1/21/2017**

Source:

The very first full day of the Trump Presidency, Sean Spicer gave us a taste of the daily bending of reality he'd attempt whenever a microphone ended up in front of his mouth. At his first Press Briefing, Sean angrily explained that contrary to all evidence, Donald Trump had the largest Inaugural crowd of all time. Period.

Sean Spicer would go on to have a truly incredible, but not enviable, record of lying during his tenure in the Trump White House. Unfortunately for Sean, he might be remembered for something worse. Melissa McCarthy's recurring Sean Spicer character on Saturday Night Live is the stuff of legend.

Many people have shown they're willing to shamelessly lie for Donald Trump. Sean wasn't even the worst liar in this position, he was just the first. The lies about crowd sizes are bad, but at least he didn't lie to us about something serious, like COVID.

TW2: Alternative Facts

Date: **1/22/2017**

Source:

Many people have shown they're willing to shamelessly lie for Donald Trump, but few seemed to enjoy doing it as much as Kellyanne Conway. Appearing to say absolutely anything to make Trump look better, Kellyanne is the inventor of "Alternative Facts", which apparently is totally different from lying. I'm actually a little bit shocked the Alternative Facts defense hasn't caught on in courtrooms across the country.

Kellyanne also gave us a history lesson on the Bowling Green Massacre, one of the worst Islamic terrorist attacks on American soil. Wait. Hold up. We're getting word the Bowling Green Massacre is in fact, Alternative Facts. It never happened, but it is something that might make Donald Trump look better, or at the very least distract us from whatever Maddening thing he is doing at the time. And if we learned one thing during the Trump Presidency, the ultimate goal here was to make Trump look good. Facts be damned.

TW3: Private Security

Date: **1/23/2017**

Source: **FAKE NEWS**

While this is totally a Fake event, it is also totally plausible, so don't feel bad if you got this one wrong. It is early on in the Trump Presidency and he most definitely was keeping "his guys" close. Anyone could easily see some early growing pains with clashes between the Secret Service and Trumps "guys".

Throughout Trump's Presidency he did start to appoint "loyal" people in positions throughout the White House, including in the Secret Service. If testimony during the January 6th Hearings are to be believed, Trump expected the Secret Service to be "his guys" when push came to shove, and although we didn't get a Trump v. Secret Service battle at the start of the Trump Presidency, we did appear to get some pushing and shoving between the two parties at the end of the Trump Presidency.

TD1: Muslim Ban

Date: **1/28/2017**

Source:

Donald Trump essentially ran on the campaign promise to completely shut off the United States of America from any outsiders… who weren't white. It didn't take him long to attempt to fulfill this promise, which is actually one of the few promises he partially accomplished. Acting unilaterally, Trump signs an Executive Order banning Muslims from 7 countries for 90 days. Later Trump would say we needed to close until we could ,"figure out what is going on", which might be something you thought to yourself multiple times during the Trump Presidency.

With this event Donald Trump gives us an early example of just how truly evil he was willing to be. He was willing to pick out a specific group of people and officially identify them as an "other" who isn't welcomed in the United States of America. Didn't even consult the other two branches of government. Just Donald Trump wielding his power in any way he wants. The Maddening Level is high.

TD2: Reality White House

Date: **1/28/2017**

Source: FAKE NEWS

We didn't actually get this event in real life, but it sure was talked about a lot as a possibility. Figuring out who to appoint in a lot of government positions doesn't seem like something Donald Trump would be able to handle. He probably doesn't even know what most of the jobs are for.

Instead of doing that work, he could have had a reality show to pick who got the appointments. He'd have writers be able to do all of the work and he'd just need to show up sometime afternoon to say a few lines before going back to watching the Fox News Cinematic Universe. He'd love it.

But who are we kidding. He didn't actually pick most of the people for those appointments anyway. At least, that is what he'd have us believe now. He barely even knew any of those people he picked to work in his Administration.

TD3: Separating Children

Date: 2/2/2017

Source:

As a part of fulfilling his campaign promise to close the United States of America to all outsiders… who aren't white, Donald Trump starts developing a policy for the border with Mexico. Since he won't be able to build all that wall at once, or at all, why not develop a whole bunch of horrible conditions at the border instead? That will surely act as a deterrent! One of the policies that would eventually be put into action was separating children from their parents as they crossed the border. We ended up with some horrific video footage of children taking care of children in what appears to be large jail cells, or as some might call them, cages.

Trump became President because he gave a whole bunch of horrible people the green light to be horrible in public. He rewarded them by doing the cruelest things possible to anyone those horrible people hated. Oh, and they didn't keep track of the kids/parent matches, so many haven't been reunited.

TS2: The Best Spy

Date: 2/18/2017
Source: FAKE NEWS

Are we sure this one isn't real? It had to have happened in some meeting that we don't have any footage of.

There are countless examples of Trump holding round table style meetings that start with everyone telling him how awesome he is. An incredible representation of the entire Trump Presidency. At once point there had to be someone in the CIA that was buttering Trump up to get something and they dropped this line on him.

"Oh, yes, Sir, Mr. President, Sir. You'd make the best spy. Probably the best spy we've ever head. It is just that you're so busy being awesome all the time, otherwise we'd definitely put you out in the field."

TD4: Trump Loves Trucks

Date: 3/23/2017
Source:

Many people will say Donald Trump acts like a Toddler on a regular basis. The evidence to support that point of view is immense, but Trump's actions when the Big Trucks came to the White House prove it true in a different way than you'd assume.

As we've learned, Trump loves things that are "huge" and generally overall "the best". During a Big Truck event at the White House, Trump couldn't contain his excitement at being able to sit in a "huge" truck that I'm sure was "the best" truck to ever truck. Donald went full toddler, climbed into the front seat of the a big truck, did a little dance, and generally seemed like he was having a great time, which isn't something I thought he was capable of doing.

While not entirely horrible and mostly ridiculous, this is an example of something Trump spent his time doing a lot of while President: Anything except actual work.

TS3: Civil Civil War

Date: 5/1/2017

Source:

Beware of anyone who claims the complexities of the universe can be solved "easily", which is one of Donald Trump's favorite ways of solving problems. There are countless examples of Trump claiming he could solve any problem, literally any problem you bring to him, quickly. He is just such a genius, he is going to solve all of your problems. It'll be great, until he actually has to do something.

Not only does Trump claim he can solve current and future complex problems, he can also solve the problems of the past. In one of those examples, here Donald Trump claims he could have helped prevent the United States Civil War. He would have just had them "talk it out", which is a really smart idea. I can't believe they didn't even think to talk it out.

Maddening. Things might get better if we stop listening to people who are selling us that everything can be fixed easily and quickly. Things are hard. We need to do the work.

TD5: Two Scoops

Date: **5/8/2017**

Source:

The President of the United States is in a weird spot. You are supposed to be a "man of the people", but yet people expect you to do more than the average person. Most Presidents try very hard to balance these two personas. Not Donald Trump.

Despite living in a gold tower, with his name on it, and having a gold toilet, somehow Donald Trump convinced the MAGA base that he is "just like you", which is mind blowing. At no point in his life has Donald Trump ever been "a man of the people" and he most certainly doesn't even pretend to be one. Instead, you get Donald Trump, the President of the United States of America demanding that while everyone else at his dinner party gets one scoop of ice cream, he gets two.

The amount of ice cream he eats doesn't really hurt that many people, but the sheer fact he does stuff like this speaks volumes.

TD6: You're Fired

Date: 5/9/2017

Source:

If you were unaware, before Donald Trump was President of the United States he was a Reality TV Star. Trump and his family had a show on NBC called The Apprentice. The point of the show was to complete a series of tasks that Donald Trump created and at the end of each episode he would "fire" one person from the competition by saying, "You're fired." In fact, "You're fired.", was pretty much Trump's catchphrase. He was known as the guy that loves to fire people, right to their face.

Apparently he must have lost his love for firing people to their face when he became President. Instead of firing FBI Director James Comey to his face, Trump did it through the media. He also waited until Comey was on a trip on the other side of the country. James Comey was investigating Trump's misconduct, so he had to go. Willing to fire people looking into your misdeeds? That is worth a few hats.

TAW1: Leaked Intelligence

Date: 5/10/2017

Source:

If this event wasn't Maddning enough when it happened, it looks way worse now.

On this date, Donald Trump met with Russian Foreign Minister Sergei Lavrov at the White House. Of course the President of the United States would meet with other world leaders in the White House, but a closed door meeting with top Russian officials while there was a ton of discussion about Trump possibly using the Russians to help win the 20216 Election is already a Maddening event. Then we found out that Trump shared Intelligence secrets with the Russians at that meeting. Then we found out the ISIS related Intelligence he shared came from the Israelis.

Since this event we've learned all about Trump's mistreatment of sensitive materials. He doesn't do any of this for us. He does it all for himself, because he is straight up Mad.

TS4: Steam Powered Navy

Date: 5/11/2017

Source:

Donald Trump likes to use a very specific strategy to try to make himself seem smart. He thinks of something very simple to solve a very complex problem, something that the average person would have tried almost immediately, and then says he is the first one to think of it. The man is a modern day genius. A very stable genius.

Only his own very stable genius words can accurately paint the picture of what he meant.

"It sounded bad to me. Digital. They have digital. What is digital? And it's very complicated. You have to be Albert Einstein to figure it out. And I said — and now they want to buy more aircraft carriers. I said what system are you going to be — 'Sir, we're staying with digital.' I said no you're not. You going to goddamned steam, the digital costs hundreds of millions of dollars more money and it's no good."

TD7: Ivanka's Friend

Date: 5/20/2017

Source: FAKE NEWS

Plenty of people who were "Friends of the Trumps" ended up in government positions. We just don't have specific verifiable evidence that one of Ivanka's Friends was appointed as the White House Liaison for Art.

We do have evidence that Rudy Giuliani's Son, Andrew H. Giuliani, was appointed as the White House Liaison for Sports. Andrew doesn't appear to have ever "sported" in his life, but there he was pulling in $95,000.00 a year to be the official White House Liaison for Sports.

Despite the fact Trump claimed he was going to hire the best people, he routinely brought on incompetent people for both serious and silly roles. The the only real quality he needed from you was an undying support for Donald Trump. You didn't actually need to do anything for the people of the United States of America, just protect Donald's ego.

TAW2: The Orb

Date: **5/21/2017**
Source:

While acting as a "Real Estate Mogul", Donald Trump's interactions with various governments from around the globe could be described as problematic at best. Those relationships only became merkier when he became President. One of them even gave as a picture straight out of a James Bond movie.

Trump, along with Egyptian President Abdel Fattah al-Sisi and King Salman bin Abdulaziz of Saudi Arabia, created a photograph that can be described in one word; Villains. While the purpose of touching this orb was to "activate" the Global Center for Combating Extremist Ideology in Riyadh, Saudi Arabia, it looks more like these guys are about to remove all puppies from the world using their magical glowing orb.

Throughout his reign, Donald Trump and his Administration would continue to have merkie interactions with many countries in the Middle East. This one isn't close to the Maddest one.

TAW3: Trump Meets Pope

Date: **5/24/2017**

Source:

One would think Donald Trump would have been accustomed to interacting with people of very high status, even before coming President of the United States. That is until you factor in the fact that Donald Trump is just a very weird person.

Trump had many interesting interactions with world leaders during his time as President, but few match his visit with Pope Francis. The entire scene looks like a funeral, with Donald Trump smiling exactly as he probably smiles during a funeral, Pope Francis looking as sad as a Pope has ever looked, and Melania and Ivanka fully dressed up as if they were going to a funeral. In reality, weird events like this one are way more preferable than his evil, villain, lovefests he had with other world leaders.

Fun side note, Trump didn't let devout Catholic White House Press Secretary Sean Spicer attend the trip to meet the Pope. He truly cares about those who care for him.

TAW4: Trump in Front

Date: 5/25/2017

Source:

When Trump was named the winner of the 2016 Presidential Election there was a lot of discussion that "President Trump" was going to be different than "Campaign Trump". All of the Mad behavior during the campaign was just part of the schtick to get elected. He was going to be totally normal now. The majesty of the office would humble him. He would rise to the occasion.

He did not rise. He doesn't even know what the word humble means. The only thing he did was prove over and over again that President Trump was just going to be Campaign Trump with actual power. At a NATO Summit in Brussels, an organization he doesn't even want the United States of America to be apart of, Trump showed us exactly how much he would not shake his "brash" campaign personality by pushing the Montenegro Prime Minister, Dusko Markovic, out of the way to ensure Trump could get a first row spot in the group picture. Trump first, always.

TS5: Covfefe

Date: **5/31/2017**

Source:

If you added up all of the time Trump spent doing specific tasks while he was President it would have to look something like this:

1. Watching Fox News Cinematic Universe
2. Twittering
3. Golfing

The first two were usually related as Trump routinely Tweeted about what he was watching on TV. The amount of consistent spelling errors and misused words in his Tweets were unfathomable. From Hamberders to Stollen Elections, if there wasn't an error in the post, it was probably a ghostwriter.

Trump was also well known to Tweet through the night. In one of those instances we got a classic Trump Twitter error: Covfefe. A normal person would delete the Tweet or explain what that means. Not Trump though. He is no normal person. Just a Mad one.

We never figured out what Covfefe means.

TW4: The Wedding Planner

Date: 6/16/2017

Source:

One verifiable example of a "Friend of the Trumps" getting a position in the government during the Trump Administration is Eric Trump's Wedding Planner. Lynne Patton had worked with the Trump family planning events since 2009, including Eric Trump's wedding, so when Trump got in the White House she was appointed to run the largest office for the United States Department of Housing and Urban Development. A position I am sure she had plenty of qualifications to fulfill.

What is that? She had no prior experience in public housing at all? She lied about going to Yale? She called a reporter Miss Piggy? Surely she must have not lasted long in this position she was clearly unqualified for. She stayed in that position until Trump left office?!

I guess in a world full of unqualified and awful people, even the most unqualified of the unqualified can fly under the radar.

TW5: The Scaramucci Era

Date: 7/21/2017
Source:

The Scaramucci Era might be the most fascinating 11 days of the Trump Presidency. On July 21, 2017 Anthony Scaramucci was named as the White House Director of Communications. His years of experience in investment banking at Goldman Sachs made him the easy pick to wrangle a chaotic President and Administration. The day his appointment was announced, the White House Press Secretary, Sean Spicer, resigns.

One of Scaramucci's first acts as Director of Communications was to give Sarah Huckabee Sanders, who would become the White House Press Secretary, a makeover. We know this because he told us during an appearance on State of the Union. His second act appears to be having what he thought was an off the record conversation with a reporter where Anthony proceeded to talk trash on basically everyone in the Trump Administration. Scaramucci's 11 chaotic days gained him fame, which might be all he wanted.

TS6: Boy Scouts & Sex Parties

Date: **7/24/2017**

Source:

It is safe to say Donald Trump doesn't have a filter when he talks. He is willing to say anything to any audience at anytime. There is no better example of this than when he gave a speech to the Boy Scouts. Trump treated this public speaking event as he treated all public speak events at the time, talking about crowd sizes and bragging about his election victory. He then discussed fighting the Washington D.C. "swamp" and how he would like to change the word to "cesspool" or "sewer". Just totally normal things to discuss while giving a talk to the Boy Scouts.

Then it got worse, of course. In an effort to give a lesson on keeping one's momentum, he describes how William Levitt sold his business and had parties with all the money he made. For a second Trump says he shouldn't tell the Boy Scouts what happened at those parties, but then he says, "Should I tell you? Should I tell you? You're Boy Scouts, but you know life. You know life." It takes a special kind of Mad person to say such a thing to children.

TAW5: Local Milk People

Date: 8/3/2017

Source:

Even though Trump says a lot of Maddening things, usually one can at least figure out what he is talking about. Not in this case. We probably won't ever know what he actually meant to communicate.

On a recorded call with Australian Prime Minister Malcolm Turnbull, Trump had an exchange about a plan for the United States of America to accept hundreds of refugees from detention centers near Australia. We'll let Trump's words speak for themselves: "I guarantee you they are bad. That is why they are in prison right now. They are not going to be wonderful people who go on to work for the local milk people."

Who are these local milk people? Do wonderful people typically work for the local milk people? Will Trump work for the local milk people after he goes to prison? We'll never get answers to these questions.

TS7: Good People Both Sides

Date: 8/15/2017
Source:

There were multiple occasions where Donald Trump had the opportunity to condemn the actions of the extremists in his base, but time and time again he refuses to do so. Trump gave those far right extremists the permission to be their terrible true selves in public and there is no putting that milk back in the cow. Maybe the local milk people could (see TAW5: Local Milk People), but Trump certainly wouldn't even try.

Hundreds of Trump's extremist supporters descended upon Charlottesville, Virginia to protest the removal of Confederate statues. In their best KKK rally impersonation, they carried lit torches as they chanted, "You will not replace us.", which is a reference to Jewish people controlling non-white people to take over the white race. After clashes with protestors led to one death, Trump claimed there were good people on both side. Very Maddening.

TD8: Don't Look at It

<u>Date:</u> 8/21/2017

<u>Source:</u>

A very large part of the process of learning about a Solar Eclipse is learning to not look at a Solar Eclipse. That knowledge is more well known than the first rule of Fight Club. It is safe to say nearly everyone on the planet is aware you shouldn't look directly at a Solar Eclipse, but not Donald Trump.

Donald, joined by Melania and Barron on a White House balcony, was outside to take in the experience of the Solar Eclipse. Each one of them had fancy protective eyewear that would allow them to look at the sun without having any damage. White Donald Trump was excitedly gesturing to the sky he was given a reminder from a staff member in the form of a "Don't Look!" shout. Donald Trump then proceeded to look directly at the Solar Eclipse without the protective eyewear he was holding. This one receives a lot of hats as it shows either his pure stupidity or his primal need to to do the opposite of what others say. Not Presidential.

TD9: Paper Towels

Date: **10/3/2017**

Source:

Now this event is classic Donald Trump Maddening behavior. It is just so stupid and yet, he thought it was a really cool thing to do. There is no way this was planned in advanced. Surly someone would have told him it was a bad idea if they knew it was going to happen. In the moment, Trump saw those paper towels and had to say to himself, “I’m going to throw these paper towels at these hurricane victims. They can use them to soak up all the water.”, and then started tossing.

Trump has multiple Hurricane related events in this book and it is really hard to figure out which one of them is more Maddening. This specific one scores high on the stupidity scale, but technically he was helping people. Not in any real way that was helpful to people, but besides tying up resources in a disaster area for a photo op, they did get paper towels and everyone can use them eventually. Due to the high stupidity score, Throwing Paper Towels to Hurricane Victims gets a lot of MAGA hats.

TAW6: Japanese Fish Food

Date: 11/6/2017

Source:

While on a trip to Japan, Trump was about to have lunch with Japanese Prime Minister Shinzo Abe when we got a glimpse into one of Trump's defining qualities. The lunch location overlooked a koi pond and Donald and Shinzo were handed boxes of fish food with small spoons. After sprinkling a few spoonfuls of food into the pond, Trump turned his box over to dump out the remaining food. Maybe he just really wanted to move on to his lunch, which is both totally acceptable and totally possible, but it is a perfect representation of his impatience.

Whether it is building a company, governing a nation, or feeding fish, Trump will give up quickly and take the easy way out. The man has no attention span and no ability to work through even the simplest of tasks. He couldn't even get through emptying a box of fish food. While this event didn't cause too much harm to others, it is emblematic of a larger problem.

TD10: Can't Drink Water

Date: 11/15/2017

Source:

Back in February of 2013 a rising star of the Republican Party, Marco Rubio, was selected to give the Republican response to Obama's State of the Union speech. Unfortunately for Marco, most people only remember his speech for one reason, his really weird way of drinking from a bottle of water. Donald Trump is most certainly one of those people. Trump regularly made fun of Marco's inability to drink water throughout the 2016 Republican Primary. Then we found out Trump also has problems drinking water from a bottle of water.

While giving a speech at the White House Trump bends over to get a bottle of water in the podium, but he finds no water. Trump tries to play this off by saying, "They don't have water. That is okay.", with a tone that insinuates it is definitely not okay. He is then told there is a bottle of water right next to him, but they would have been way better off not telling him. Opening it was weird. The first sip was weird. The second sip is Maddening.

TS8: Invisible F-35s

Date: **11/23/2017**

Source:

The F-35 is arguably the best fighter jet in the history of the world. One of the distinguishing features of the F-35 is the stealth features it possesses. Those features make it the best fighter jet to evade enemy detection and enter contested airspaces. While the stealth capabilities are beyond incredible, it is not literally invisible, but you try to explain that to Donald J. Trump, President of the United States and Commander in Chief of the Armed Forces.

This date in history wasn't even the first time Trump mentioned that the F-35 was invisible, but it is the date we have proof of him saying it was invisible. Literally.

"You like the F-35? ... You can't see it. You literally can't see it. It's hard to fight a plane you can't see."

TAW7: Nuke North Korea Tweet

Date: **1/2/2018**

Source:

Hillary Clinton warned us during a 2016 Presidential Debate with these words, "A man you can bait with a Tweet is not a man we can trust with nuclear weapons." Trump couldn't even make it through the first year of his Presidency before he was baited into using Twitter to threaten using nuclear weapons.

Donald Trump's relationship with Kim Jong Un and North Korea may have ended strong, but things were a bit dicey at the start. To kick off the new year, Kim Jong Un did what every leader of North Korea has alway done; Threaten the United States with weapons that are totally, for sure, going to reach them this time. Every other American President has done what a normal human would do when they make proclamations like this, ignore them. Unfortunately, Donald Trump is no normal person. Donald Tweeted that he too has a Nuclear Button that is "much bigger and more powerful button", because of course he did.

TW6: The Wolff of White House

Date: 1/5/2018

Source:

As we approached the one year mark of the Trump Presidency we received one of our first real insider looks at what was really going on in the White House. In *Fire and Fury: Inside the Trump White House*, Michael Wolff details some Mad stuff, like Trump getting bored when they tried to teach him the Constitution. You know the Constitution, the thing Trump swore to defend less than a year before.

Michael Wolff interviewed people in Trump World during the 2016 campaign and ended up with West Wing access at the start of the Trump Administration. From there he just hung around. He took notes. He interviewed a few people. Then he wrote a book. Eventually the Trump White House would claim it was Steve Bannon who provided Wolff the access and no really knew why he was there. A+ effort on letting random people roam the White House, but this event has a positive spin as it is one of the first pieces of evidence that the Trump Administration was every bit as Mad as we assumed.

TW7: Drunk Doctor

Date: **1/16/2018**

Source:

Dr. Ronny Jackson had been a Rear Admiral in the Navy and was the Physician to the President from 2013-2018. Then he met Donald J. Trump.

After giving Trump a physical, Dr. Jackson gave a one hour press conference to detail how amazing Donald Trump is. In that hour he claimed Trump has "excellent genes" and that Trump could live to be 200 years old. The Donald Trump love fest was topped off by Trump allegedly coming in at 6'3 and weighing 239 pounds. One more inch smaller or one more pound heavier and Donald would technically be "obese", which is news he'd definitely not take well.

Thanks to his glowing review of Trump as a physical specimen, Dr. Jackson was nominated to be the Secretary of Veteran Affairs. He would quickly withdraw as news broke of him regularly being drunk and on sleeping pills while on the job. He is now a member of the US House of Representatives, as a member of the Republican caucus.

TAW8: Trump No More

Date: 3/5/2018

Source:

While this event certainly didn't negatively impact others, it is probably the event that hurt Donald Trump the most. There are few things he loves more in life than the Trump Brand, which is interesting considering the Trump Brand is filled with failures. For example: An Airline, Bottled Water, Casinos, a Magazine, Steaks, Vodka, and a University. His love for the Trump Brand, as we found out in his Trump Org Fraud case, even causes him to overvalue anything with "Trump" attached to it.

Despite a lot of Trump branded products failing, he has been able to put together a respectable portfolio of Trump branded buildings. Although, much like Icarus, Trump flew too close to the sun by becoming President. His divisiveness led a large portion of the world to boycott anything with the name Trump attached. Buildings all over the world began to remove their Trump branding from their facades in scenes that are reminiscent of statues of Saddam Hussein being toppled in Iraq.

TW8: Drunk Nunberg

Date: **3/5/2018**

Source:

Although he was eventually let go from any "official" capacity due to a Tweet he posted with a racial slur, Sam Nunberg had been a member of Trump World since the 2016 Presidential Campaign. Sam's presence throughout that time made him a key witness in the Muller Investigation into Russia's meddling into the 2016 Election. After it was reported he was subpoenaed to appear before the grand jury investigating Russia's interference, Sam thought it was a good idea to go on a bunch of cable news shows.

Throughout his appearances he made some interesting statements. He said he was going to refuse to comply with the subpoena, claimed "Trump may have done something" with Russia during the 2016 Election, and stated Carter Page colluded with the Russian's to help get Trump elected. As he went from one show to the next, each host eventually noticed Sam appeared to be drunk. MSNBC's Katy Tur even called him out on live on TV for smelling like alcohol. Another example of Trump hiring the "best" people.

TD11: Two More Days

Date: **3/16/2018**

Source:

One of Donald Trump's key personality traits is his need to get revenge against those who he has deemed his enemy. One of the largest groups of his "enemies"includes anyone who attempts to hold Trump accountable for his actions. During this time of his Presidency, Trump was finding "enemies" all over the place as there were multiple investigations into his actions taken during the 2016 Presidential Campaign.

Andrew McCabe, who was the Deputy Director of the FBI, was one of Trump's many "enemies". Ten months before this date, McCabe had opened one of the investigations into Donald Trump. On this day though, he was only two days away from officially retiring from his position with the FBI. To get his revenge against McCabe, Trump had then Attorney General Jeff Sessions fire McCabe to block him from getting his pension. McCabe did eventually get his pension fully restored, but firing those who are investigating you is a real dictator move.

TW9: Trump, Cohen, Hannity

Date: 4/16/2018

Source:

Donald Trump typically relies on gathering people around him who will protect him at all cost. A vast majority of those people end up being apart of his ever growing team of lawyers. The most famous of this group may be Michael Cohen, who started working for Trump in 2006. Everything was working great between Trump and Cohen until early 2018 and their relationship has only deteriorated since as Cohen "flipped" on Trump and has admitted to committing multiple crimes for him.

As a part of his legal troubles stemming from his work for Trump, Michael Cohen ended up in a few different courtrooms. In this specific case he was trying to withhold the name of one of his clients. Cohen even attempted to submit the name to the Judge via a sealed envelope. Turned out the client was Sean Hannity, one of the top hosts of the Fox News Cinematic Universe, aka the Trump Propaganda Network. Only a few hats until we figure out why this information was needed to be a secret.

TAW9: Fast Food International

Date: **6/7/2018**

Source: **FAKE NEWS**

Donald Trump's love of fast food is well documented, but as far as we know, he did not bring McDonald's with him to the G7 Summit in Canada. Is it possible that he did bring McDonald's with him? Absolutely. We just don't have any clear evidence or sources connecting him to this specific event.

Based on all available information, one could assume Donald Trump would not like any of the fancy food served at events like the G7 Summit. We have documented evidence he only likes his steaks well done with ketchup, no way he likes Haute Cuisine. Additionally, one could assume he isn't smart enough to know he could just get McDonald's in Canada and he would talk straight through someone trying to explain that to him.

While fake, this isn't even the Maddest Fast Food related Trump event of his Presidency. Two hats.

TAW10: World Leader Scold

Date: **6/9/2018**

Source:

It is safe to assume many world leaders do not have a favorable view of Donald Trump. A lot of them are serious humans who are trying to do the best for their country, which is the complete opposite of Donald Trump. Having to deal with him to handle regular, everyday normal problems is a chore, but dealing with him to collaboratively solve the problems of the world has to be infuriating.

On June 9, 2018 we got a glimpse of just how infuriated those world leaders get when having to deal with Trump. A group of clearly frustrated world leaders including German Chancellor Angela Merkel, French President Emmanuel Macron, and Japanese Prime Minister Shinzo Abe stand on one side of a table as President of the United States Donald J. Trump sits on the other side doing the best impression of a toddler of all time. It was once thought that the Office of the Presidency would change Trump. This picture proves that thought false.

TD12: Shredding Docs

Date: 6/10/2018
Source:

Probably out of habit from his illegal dealings with his business, while President of the United States, Donald Trump would regularly rip up documents during meetings. Unfortunately, all of the documents Trump would rip into "tiny pieces" fall under the Presidential Records Act which means they need to be preserved and sent to the National Archives as historical records. Since no one could stop him from ripping up these documents, they had to take a different approach.

Aides to President Trump would collect the ripped up pieces of paper from his desk and floor, then send them to a team who would put the documents back together using tape before sending them to the National Archives. You can't make this up.

If Donald Trump did this with ALL of the documents he came across during his time as President he might not be facing criminal charges for mishandling classified documents.

TAW11: Saluting North Koreans

Date: 6/14/2018

Source:

A major aspect of Trump's campaign to be President focused on the idea of American Exceptionalism. He was going to MAGA, Make America Great Again, and put America first. This attitude was so prevalent in his campaign that parody videos started to emerge from other countries conceding that America was first, but asking Trump if their country could be second. Additionally, Trump claimed to love and respect the men and women of the United States Armed Forces as they were the people who keep America safe.

After all of that, Donald Trump, whether because he is just a weird person or because he lies to get whatever he wants, ends up saluting a North Korean Military General at a meeting with Kim Jong Un. The picture of any United States President saluting anyone outside of the United States Armed Forces is going to draw some negative attention. To salute a member of the North Korean dictatorship regime is Maddening. It will always be Trump First.

TAW12: Where is the Queen?

Date: 7/13/2018

Source:

The British have a lot of rules and regulations to follow when meeting their monarch. Men only bow with their head and women are expected to curtsey. You should refer to them as "Your Majesty" and don't start eating before they do. Furthermore, it is frowned upon to touch the monarch and you most certainly never turn your back on them. That is, unless you are Donald Trump.

While on a visit to meet Queen Elizabeth, Donald Trump and the Queen participated in a walk where they were "Inspecting the Guard of Honour" and Trump behaved exactly how you might imagine. In the video, Trump doesn't appear to know where he is going or what he is supposed to do. The Queen attempts to give him some guidance on where they are going and somehow Trump ends up walking directly in front of the Queen, wanders for a bit, and then stops leaving the Queen trying to find a way around him. This sort of behavior shouldn't be surprising. He doesn't respect our own culture, either.

TAW13: Pay Me to Protect Me

Date: 7/14/2018

Source:

Always be Grifting: The Donald Trump Story

Although Donald Trump and his kids have reportedly denied making money off of the Trump Presidency, all evidence points to them making out like the grifting bandits they are. As President, Trump went back to the grifting horse that brought him there, bringing in large sums of money through his buildings. The Trump family made huge amounts of money from the Trump D.C. hotel as they charged higher than market rate for rooms which gave you direct access to the President. That is Mad, but at least it wasn't our tax money.

Instead, our tax money went to paying the Secret Service to protect Trump at his own properties, like this stay at his Trump Turnberry Resort in Scotland. Wherever and whenever he could, Trump charged the very organization tasked with saving his life, on our dime, to protect him at places he owned. We paid Donald Trump to protect Donald Trump.

TD13: No Notes

Date: 7/16/2018

Source:

It is impossible to review the Trump Presidency without talking about Russia, a lot. Through the efforts of multiple investigations we have an embarrassing amount of evidence pointing to Trump working with Russia to help get him elected in 2016. By this point in his reign there were bright lights shining on all of the connections between the two. Surely Trump wouldn't hold a one on one meeting with Russian President Vladimir Putin in the middle of that scrutiny.

Oh, that is right! He did. It is reported Trump and Putin have met five times. Two of those meetings were private, but this is the only one that had just Trump, Putin, and a Translator. As close to a one on one meeting as the two could get. And then Trump ensured no one would ever get to know what was really said in that meeting. He took the Translators notes. Definitely something an innocent person does.

TAW14: Yes, Master Putin

Date: 7/16/2018

Source:

After meeting with Russian President Vladimir Putin, Donald Trump and Putin held a joint press conference which led to perhaps the most pathetic display of not just the entire Trump Presidency, but of any Presidency. While walking into the press conference it appeared as though Donald Trump was literally cowering to Putin. They had just finished a private one on one meeting and Trump's body language alone spoke volumes as to what was discussed behind those close doors.

While pathetic enough, that visual wasn't the worst thing to come from Trump at this press conference. When pressed about Russia's involvement with the 2016 Election, Trump sided with Putin.

"President Putin says it's not Russia. I don't see any reason why it would be."

Not great, Donald. Not great, at all.

TS9: Need ID?

Date: 7/31/2018
Source:

Donald J. Trump has not led a normal life. From the moment Trump was born he was in a sheltered world of wealth. This has caused him to have a few odd theories about what happens in the "real" world. For instance, Donald Trump believes people have a finite "battery" and if you exercise too much you'll drain your "battery" early and die. Even weirder, he thinks one should eat pizza with a fork.

An additional weird theory about the "real" world Trump believes is that people need to use an ID to buy groceries. Although, this weird belief might be one of the many things Trump lies about for nefarious purposes. Republicans seem to be well aware of the fact that if more people vote, they lose. They've tried everything possible to limit the ability for people to vote, including enacting Voter ID laws. Donald Trump blames his election loses on "Voter Fraud", so at least in his mind, if you need an ID to buy groceries, you need an ID to Vote. The REAL world begs to differ.

TD14: National Golf Day

Date: **8/4/2018**

Source: **FAKE NEWS**

Donald Trump owns multiple properties with golf courses and he spent a reported 307 days golfing while President of the United States. That means he spent 21% of his time as the leader of the United States on the golf course. That statistic alone makes it believable that Trump would institute a National Golf Day. It is even more likely he would create it on this specific date, Obama's Birthday. Alas, Trump could not find the time to proclaim a National Golf Day.

Incredibly, Pre-President Trump had some strong comments about a President's availability to play golf while President. In 2014 Trump said, "Can you believe that, with all of the problems and difficulties facing the U.S., President Obama spent the day playing golf. Worse than Carter." On the campaign trail in 2016 Trump claimed, "I'm going to be working for you, I'm not going to have time to go play golf."

Four hats for this fictitious event, because he for sure would have made it Obama's Birthday.

TD15: Farmer Trump

Date: **9/2/2018**

Source: **FAKE NEWS**

Trump going to a farm at all isn't believable, but if someone was able to get him to a farm he most definitely would just watch as other people did work. The man hasn't done a single second of manual labor in his life, he certainly isn't going to start while his President of the United States of America.

While not real, this is a good spot to go over how badly Trump hurt farmers during his reign. Despite his continually claims that he has done a great job for farmers, his overall record for the industry is abysmal. As a part of his rush to undo everything Obama did, Trump quickly rescinded guidelines the Obama Administration put in place to protect livestock farmers from agricultural monopolies. Additionally, Trump was very excited about his trade war with China, but it had a huge impact on the agricultural industry in the United States. Iowa alone lost $1.7 billion due to Trump's trade war as they their corn, soybean, and hog industry took a huge hit without the buyers from China.

TD16: Big Men Always Crying

Date: 9/7/2018
Source:

Donald Trump loves to make things up, so much so it is reported he lied 30,573 times over the four years he was President of the United States of America. That is around 20 lies everyday! Some of the things he makes up end up being extremely harmful to large groups of people, but he doesn't even just lie about the big stuff. He lies about small things that serve no real purpose, all the time.

One of the small lies he continually tells is stories about "Big, Strong Men" always crying to him while they explain how Trump has made their lives better. This lie is always told during some sort of political rally Trump is holding and follow the same pattern. Trump comes out to talk about whatever he was there to talk about and before getting distracted by complaining about something else, he tells the same anecdote about these big, strong men, who have never cried before in their lives, came up to him before his speech to tell him, with tears in their eyes, how Trump saved them. His weirdness is Maddening.

TS10: Wet Hurricanes

<u>Date:</u> 9/18/2018

<u>Source:</u>

Donald J. Trump has the best words. We know this because during a campaign event for the 2016 Presidential Election he told us. He said, “I went to an Ivy League school. I’m very highly educated. I know words. I have the best words.” Throughout his reign as President of the United States, Donald Trump would provide ample evidence to prove he does in fact not know words, let alone have the best words. The best evidence we have to make this claim might be when he described hurricanes as “wet”.

Before taking a trip to North Carolina to survey the damage caused by Hurricane Florence Trump thanked the first responders who were helping deal with the aftermath. He described Hurricane Florence as being “the wettest we have ever seen, from the standpoint of water”. This statement was pre-recorded. They could have done a second take.

The best words.

TAW15: Stand Up at the UN

Date: 9/25/2018

Source:

A major aspect of Donald Trump's message while running for President of the United States of America was that the USA was no longer respected on the world stage, but he, and he alone, could restore that respect. He would claim, on a regular basis, "The world is going to respect us again. Believe me." That claim was proven false throughout multiple international trips during the first two years of his reign, but it would be at event on US soil where it was really driven home that Donald Trump was not in fact respected on the world stage.

On September 25, 2018, Trump earnestly walked to the podium to delivery remarks to the United Nations. This was one of the few times in his Presidency Trump appeared to be trying to act serious, but it would take only one minute for Trump to make an outlandish claim that garnered laughs from members of the UN. A literal LOL moment.

If Donald Trump says, "Believe me.", don't.

TAW16: Trump Hearts Un

Date: **9/29/2018**
Source:

For essentially their entire existence, North Korea has viewed the United States of America as an enemy. Every so often they make vague threats about how they could totally destroy the USA if they wanted to and most American Presidents have smartly ignored their boasts. Unfortunately, Donald Trump is not most American Presidents. He continually responded, threateningly, to Kim Jong Un over official channels like Twitter, but like almost every Rom-Com in history, Trump's relationship with North Korea may have started off rocky at best, but through a series of shenanigans they ended up falling in love.

In a rare moment of lucidity, Trump explained the relationship well, "I was really being tough - and so was he. And we would go back and forth, And then we fell in love, okay? No, really - he wrote me beautiful letters, and they're great letters." Nothing like his own words to help show all one really needs to do to get Trump to like you is tell him you like him. Not Presidential behavior. Maddening behavior.

TS11: New White House

Date: **10/7/2018**

Source: **FAKE NEWS**

It is definitely not your fault if you got this one wrong. Donald Trump one billion percent had to have talked about this with someone, we just don't have any specific evidence to prove it. Although, it is not like a lack of evidence has ever stopped Donald Trump or his cult followers from believing things are real before.

Donald Trump is well known to be addicted to utilizing a Maddening amount of extravagant hyperbole to describe everything he does. Everything he does is always the "best", in whatever way that fits the situation. Descriptions of his real estate properties are no exception to this rule. His addiction to this is so bad that after the terrorist attacks in New York City on 9/11/2001 he claimed his building was now the tallest building in downtown Manhattan.

With that sort of Madness, living in the White House wouldn't be enough. He surely would have tried to make it bigger, taller, better. The Best.

TD17: Kanye in the Oval

Date: **10/11/2018**

Source:

Visiting the Oval Office is very rare. It is a serious place, for serious business and important meetings. Unless you're Donald Trump. Instead, you utilize the room for Photo Ops with all sorts of people, who of course most definitely did not pay for the opportunity… Who could ever forget the time Trump took pictures in the Oval Office, at the Resolute Desk, with important, serious people such as Sarah Palin, Ted Nugent, Kid Rock, and Diamond and Silk.

Among these important, serious people who visited Trump in the Oval Office is Kanye West. The meeting can best be summed up with Ye's own words referencing the MAGA hat he wore, "It was something about when I put this hat on, it made me feel like Superman." Since this visit, Kanye would only go further and further into conspiracy land, attempted a run for President in 2020, and would eventually make antisemitic remarks. He also visited Trump post Presidency at Mar-a-Lago with a well known White Supremacists.

TD18: Big Member Toilet AG

Date: 11/7/2018
Source:

The United States Attorney General (AG) is the leader of the United States Department of Justice. Essentially, the AG is the lawyer for the American people. As per usual, Donald Trump had a different view of this position a little differently, he saw the position of AG as his lawyer. As a reward for being one of his first vocal supporters, Donald Trump appointed Jeff Sessions as Attorney General.

Eventually the relationship would sour between the two after Sessions recused himself from overseeing the investigation into the Russia-Trump connections during the 2016 Election. Trump would eventually fire Session for not being loyal. Clearly Sessions should have just shut down the investigation to protect Trump. For Trump's next AG he would surely need someone more loyal to him. He turned to someone who was publicly protecting Trump, Matthew Whitaker, noted scam artist and peddler of toilets for "well endowed" men.

TS12: Suckers and Losers

Date: **11/10/2018**

Source:

Donald Trump is, as he says, a huge fan of the United States of America and he has the deepest respect for the people who protect and serve the USA. All of his words and actions say otherwise. Donald Trump did everything he could, even enduring bone spurs, to avoid being one of the honorable people who protect and serve the USA. His refusal to sacrifice for the United States of America is bad, but his thoughts on those that do is even worse.

We have evidence of the multiple times Donald Trump has disrespected US service members, including not wanting wounded soldiers at his parades because they will make him look weak. Here he calls them "losers" and "suckers" for dying for their country. The hypocrisy and ensuing mind bending cognitive dissonance contained within this event is too high to be calculated. Almost broke the Madness scale. Definitely a top 5 worst thing Trump has ever said, arguably number 1.

TAW17: Rain? I'm Out.

Date: 11/10/2018

Source:

Donald appears to have a true disdain for those who serve the United States of America, but end up getting hurt or killed in the process. This disdain probably stems from them doing something way beyond Trump's ability to understand sacrificing something for someone else. In the Trump Alternate Universe, sacrificing something for someone else is a sign of weakness. If only you were smarter or tougher, you wouldn't need to make those sacrifices.

Trump showed a great representation of his thoughts on the topic when he was scheduled to go to a World War 1 memorial service in Paris with a bunch of other world leaders. Unfortunately, it was raining. The inconvenience of getting wet is beyond what Trump is willing to sacrifice to honor those who sacrificed their lives for their countries. Trump claimed he couldn't attend the memorial service because the helicopter couldn't fly in the rain and the Secret Service wouldn't drive him. He was the only world leader scheduled to be there to not attend.

TW10: Creepy Christmas

Date: 11/26/2018
Source:

Due to the bubble of wealth that has always surrounded the Trump's, they have an interesting take on what "good style" means. This leads the Trumps to live out a lifestyle that can be described as what poor people think rich people act like. Before going to the White House they lived in a Penthouse Apartment in Trump Tower that was covered in 24-carat gold. The gold even extended all the way to the toilet.

Due to their ideas of what constitutes good design, the Christmas decorations at the White House never stood a chance and 2018's display somehow one upped 2017's display, which included a hallway filled with potted white sticks. Both sides, just absolutely filled with 10+ foot tall sticks in pots. While scary, it wasn't creepy enough for the Trumps. In 2018, Meliana, who was in charge of the decorating, went with the theme of "American Treasures". This theme included replacing the potted sticks with Christmas Tree shaped decorations made of berries, which were blood red. A blood red Christmas hallway.

TS13: Do You Still Believe?

Date: **12/24/2018**

Source:

It is a tradition for the President and First Lady to receive calls from children on Christmas Eve. They sit in front of a nicely decorated fireplace in the White House and take a few phone calls to discuss Christmas with the kids while some members of the press memorialize the event in pictures and videos. What could possibly go wrong? Oh, that is right. We're talking about Donald Trump. Of course something could go wrong.

On Christmas Eve in 2018, Donald Trump received a phone call from a seven year old. Trump, not being Mad at all and totally knowing how to interact with kids, proceeds to ask the child if they still believed in Santa Claus. Yes, this actually happened. Trump said, "Are you still a believer in Santa? Because at 7, it's marginal, right?" Marginal? He expected this seven year old to no longer believe in Santa and know the meaning of the word "marginal"? Has he ever met a kid before? One should probably be able to act semi-normal around children to be President.

TD19: Fast Food Champs

Date: **1/14/2019**

Source:

Many championship teams, both professional and amatuer, are invited to the White House. This tradition was hit or miss during Donald Trump's time as President of the United States as whole teams would not attend in protest of his aggressive, cruel, and Maddening style of governing. Since Trump can't take being turned down, he eventually stopped even offering White House visits to leagues and teams who were vocally anti-Trump.

Fortunately for the Clemson Football team, the National College Football Championships, Donald Trump felt they were worthy enough of an invitation. After all, they do hail from a state that voted for him. Donald Trump rewarded these top athletes during their visit by giving them a buffet. A buffet filled with fast food. Granted there was a government shutdown at the time, which was his fault, but at least he claimed he paid for the food. Which we're sure is 100% true and totally not a lie. Just as true as Trump's ability to spell "Hamberders" correctly.

TS14: Tim Apple, CEO of Cook

Date: 3/6/2019
Source:

Donald Trump has a Maddening relationship with the names of other people. Sometimes he forgets their names and tries to power through by going with whatever he thinks their name is. It is explains why he comes up with nicknames for everyone, which are always mean spirited because he has probably never had a positive thought about another person in his life.

In this case, it was not his normal environment for forgetting names. He is usually mid speech at a rally where he gets easily distracted and goes off the cuff. Those types of episodes have led to Trump calling even his most ardent supporters by the wrong name. For instance, he once called Matt Gaetz, professional troll of the House GOP, Rick Gates. Rick Gates, by the way, is a former Trump aide who plead guilty to conspiring with Russia to help Trump win the 2016 Election. This time, Tim Cook was sitting with a name plate directly in front of him and Trump still got his name wrong.

TAW18: Trump Pisa

Date: 3/27/2019
Source: FAKE NEWS

Donald Trump has a penchant for claiming to be able to solve all sorts of problems. He is even well known for saying the phrase, "I alone can fit it.", and claiming to be able to solve these problems incredibly easily. It is probably because he says he knows more about a lot of subjects than anyone else. Just a few examples of his self proclaimed areas of expertise include Drones, Technology, Drone Technology, Infrastructure, Renewable Energy, Lawsuits, Courts, ISIS, TV Ratings, Campaign Finance, and Senator Cory Booker who Trump says he knows better than Cory knows himself.

While we know Trump has visited Italy, we don't evidence he has visited the Leaning Tower of Pisa. Although, just because he has never been there before doesn't mean he never said he could fix it. One thing we know for sure, if Trump was to offer to fix it he would demand to have his name attached to it. The Trump Tower of Pisa is right up his alley.

TW11: Fantastic Mr. Kushner

Date: 4/1/2019

Source:

In what seems like a great April Fools' Day prank, it is April 1, 2019 when we learned that Jared Kushner, Ivanka's husband and Donald Trump's son in law, was denied a security clearance to work in the White House over concerns of being at risk for foreign influence. Instead of moving forward as everyone else would, not providing him a security clearance and a job in the White House, Donald Trump overrode that denial and made sure Jared Kushner got any security clearance he needed and a job in the White House.

Jared's job in the Trump Administration didn't really have a title other than Senior Advisor to the President, but that was probably because he was involved in everything. His expertise seemed to range from Healthcare to Border Infrastructure to bringing peace to the Middle East. In the final days of the Trump Presidency he was in charge of selling pardons. Oh, and just after the Trump Administration ended he received $2 billion from a Saudi investment firm run by their crown prince. The grift of all grifts.

TS15: Windmill Cancer

Date: 4/2/2019
Source:

The Republican party has made it blatantly clear they are against renewable energy sources. While they are against all forms of renewable energy, they have a special hatred for windmills. Windmills harness the power of the wind, a rather constant presence on Earth, and would help provide a valuable renewable source of energy across the globe. There are two main problems Republicans have with them. First, you have to look at them. Second, their Big Oil overload donors would lose a ton of profits.

Rather than admitting to either of those, Republicans will go to great lengths to bad mouth windmills. They'll claim they kill wildlife, which is apparently vastly different from the world being destroyed by a continued reliance on fossil fuels. As per usual, Donald Trump took things a bit further by saying, "If you have a windmill anywhere near your house, congratulations, your house just went down 75 percent in value. And they say the noise causes cancer." Yup. That actually happened.

Get McCain Out of Here

Date: 5/28/2019
Source:

John McCain was a US Senator and the Republican Nominee for President in 2008. Additionally, John served in the United States Navy during the Vietnam War where he would become a prisoner of war for six years. John McCain was willing to sacrifice everything inservice to the United States of America. McCain is famous for stopping a woman at a town hall event from bad mouthing Barack Obama and being the deciding vote in the Senate to stop Trump's attempt to repeal the Affordable Care Act, also known as Obama Care. Furthermore, he refused to endorse Trump for President.

Any one of those events would cause Trump to put McCain on his enemies list. Not only had he continually done what Trump could never do, honorably serve the people of the United States of America, he had also publicly stood up to Trump. Trump hates this man he could never be so much, he demanded a naval ship baring the McCain name be moved so he didn't have to see it.

TS16: The Moon & Mars

Date: 6/7/2019

Source:

Just a few month early Trump Tweeted, "Under my Administration, we are restoring @NASA to greatness and we are going back to the Moon, then Mars. I am updating my budget to include an additional $1.6 billion so that we can return to Space in a BIG WAY!" Then Trump watched the Fox Cinematic Universe and Neil Cavuto told his audience, which includes Donald Trump, "...didn't we do this moon thing quite a few decades ago?"

Thanks to Neil, Trump changed his tune on going to the moon and revealed to us his excellent knowledge of all things space by Tweeting, "For all of the money we are spending, NASA should NOT be talking about going to the Moon - We did that 50 years ago. They should be focused on the much bigger things we are doing, including Mars (of which the Moon is a part), Defense and Science!" To clarify, the Moon is not apart of Mars. Trump, and now probably his cult, too, are the only ones to believe this.

TW12: Ivanka, Serious Politician

Date: 6/29/2019
Source:

Donald Trump brought a lot of severely unqualified people with him to work in the White House and Ivanka Trump may have been the most visible one of them all. At times, people referred to Ivanka as the "First Lady". While she may not have been the First Lady, she certainly attempted to put herself in a position to be seen as a vital member of the Trump Administration. She even took a picture in the Oval Office while sitting behind the Resolute Desk.

As a part of this act, Ivanka routinely attended meetings and summits with world leaders where she would attempt to be taken seriously. Unfortunately for her, the world leaders were having none of it. We ended up getting a classic piece of evidence of this in action at the G20 Summit in Japan. A video emerged of a Ivanka trying to jump into a conversation between French President Emmanuel Macron, British Prime Minister Theresa May, and Canadian Prime Minister Justin Trudeau, but despite her attempts, Ivanka was categorically ignored.

TS17: Revolutionary War Planes

Date: 7/4/2019

Source:

After attending a Bastille Day parade, Donald Trump demanded a parade of his own on July 4th. Trump wasn't able to get everything he wanted, but he was able to get a July 4th celebration in Washington, D.C. which allowed him to be the center of the attention and that is all he really wanted anyway. Unfortunately for Donald, it rained the whole day in D.C.

Donald Trump pushed through the inconvenience of being wet so he could give a speech on the grounds of the Lincoln Memorial. Trump's team had erected a series of fences and barriers to ensure no one could get too close to the President. This set up led to Trump reading his speech from a teleprompter at a distance, through a raindrop covered bullet proof barrier. Trump got lost in his speech and ended up saying the Americans took airports from the British during the Revolutionary War. No matter how lost one gets in a speech, that is a Mad place to end up.

TS18: Quid Pro Quo

Date: 7/25/2019

Source:

As the 2020 Election cycle was starting to kick into gear, Donald Trump dipped back into his old bag of tricks. In an attempt to get foreign countries to make his potential opponents look bad, Donald Trump offered up a Quid Pro Quo to the President of Ukraine, Volodymyr Zelenskyy.

On a recorded phone call with Zelenskyy, the day after Muller delivered his findings of the Russia-Trump 2016 election probe, Donald Trump pressed the Ukrainian President to open an investigation into Joe Biden's potential involvement with his son Hunter's work with a Ukrainian gas company. If they could at least say they were investigating, Trump's team would take care of the rest and Zelenskyy would be offered a White House visit and defense support from the United States. This event ended with Trump's first impeachment and gets worse as time goes on as Russia continues to attack Ukraine. Trump will most definitely side with Russia in a potential second term in office.

TAW19: Buying Greenland

Date: 8/18/2019
Source:

This one might not actually be that bad of an idea, it is just that it is an absolutely Mad thing to do in this day and age. The last time the United States of America bought land from another country was Denmark in 1916. Donald Trump turned to the same country to revive this ancient practice by attempting to buy Greenland.

Donald Trump defended his efforts to buy Greenland from Denmark by likening it to a "large real estate deal", something that is right in Trump's wheel house. While mostly covered with ice, Trump wasn't necessarily wrong in his thinking that Greenland would be a strategic value for the United States. Very rarely is having more territory a detriment, so depending on the price it might not be that Mad. Donald Trump doesn't seem to have a great track record with handling finances though, so he would most likely have gotten ripped off if Denmark wanted to play ball. Not a Mad idea, but the execution of the plan would have been very Maddening.

TS19: Nuke Hurricanes

Date: **8/25/2019**

Source:

Donald Trump claims to be one of the smartest people of all time. He has stated multiple times that he has a "large brain", even going as far as saying China respects him for his "very, very large brain". Unfortunately for basically everyone, Trump has yet to prove his "large" brain actually makes him smart. Instead, he seems to think of really bad ideas that other people have already discarded and thus never talked about, and says them as if he is the first one to ever think of them.

In this case, Donald Trump pondered why we can't just Nuke Hurricanes. This date provided us with the first report we have for this Maddening suggestion. Trump allegedly said, "...as they're moving across the Atlantic, we drop a bomb inside the eye of the hurricane and it disrupts it. Why can't we do that?" This statement also gave us one of the best quotes from the Trump Presidency as the source for this story said, "You could hear a gnat fart in that meeting. People were astonished."

TD21: Hurricane Paths

Date: 9/4/2019
Source:

Donald J. Trump has never been wrong a day in his life. At least, according to Donald J. Trump. He displays this belief on a regular basis, especially when he is giving speeches and messes up saying a word. He immediately repeats the wrong word followed by the right word and then says something to the effective of "them, too" as if the mispronounced word was meant to be included. Donald J. Trump never makes mistakes.

A great example of this behavior in action was when he drew an extra hurricane path on an official National Oceanic and Atmospheric Administration projection path for Hurricane Dorian. Early on in the projections for where Hurricane Dorian could go, Donald Trump said the people of Alabama should be prepared. The problem is Alabama wasn't actually in the path of the hurricane. Since Donald J. Trump is never wrong and doesn't make mistakes, Trump took a large black Sharpie to an official map to make himself right. Only a Mad person would do this.

TAW20: Trump & the Taliban

Date: **9/7/2019**

Source: **FAKE NEWS**

This Fake event actually starts off as a Real event, but the second part never happened. At least that we know of.

On this date, Trump announced that he had indeed invited the Taliban to come meet with him at Camp David. Yes, that Taliban. Just four days before the anniversary of 9/11. Every so often, even Donald Trump caves to public pressure and canceled the meeting at Camp David with the Taliban.

One can only assume what Donald Trump's play was here, but we might assume he just likes their style. The Taliban is very clearly on the "enemy" side for the United States of America, but that didn't stop Donald Trump from cozying up to other classic USA "enemies" such as Russia and North Korea. They all seem to have one factor in common; a leader who is able to do whatever they want, whenever they want. Sounds exactly like the type of person Trump would try to emulate, regardless of their atrocities.

TAW21: ISIS Leader, Died Like a Dog

Date: **10/26/2019**

Source:

The 2011 White House Correspondents' Association dinner was held on May 1, 2011. Barack Obama was President and Donald Trump was in attendance. At the time, Trump had made multiple negative remarks about Obama, including questioning his place of birth. Obama responded by eviscerating Trump during his speech, including the line, “These are the kind of decisions that would keep me up at night.”, when referring to Trump’s decisions on who to fire on The Apprentice. Within 24 hours, Obama would oversee the operation that killed Osama Bin Laden and delivered a somber speech to the American people detailing this momentous event.

On this date, Trump would oversee the operation that killed the leader of ISIS and proceeded to try to match Obama’s speech from May 2, 2011. Shockingly, he did not do a great job. His speech was truly unhinged. Scan this additional QR Code to see a direct comparison for yourself.

TS20: No One Can Dock

Date: 3/6/2020

Source:

Many of the events in the COVID era score very high in the Madness Rankings because Donald Trump was clearly making decisions that he thought would make him look better at the expense of people dying. While it was clear to see his true strategy playout in real time, it would become even worse once we got the evidence, in the form of recorded interviews, where he admitting to knowing the seriousness of the situation. He just didn't care.

Before COVID would completely cripple the United States of America for an extended period of time, Donald Trump was making decisions in an attempt to hide just how serious the problem was going to be. It started with him not wanting the Grand Princess cruise ship to dock in San Francisco as 35 people had reported "flu-like symptoms". Trump claimed he didn't want them to dock because, "I don't need to have the numbers double because of one ship that wasn't our fault." Truly Madding Leadership.

TW13: Vegetables Cause Covid

Date: **3/13/2020**

Source: **FAKE NEWS**

Donald Trump is willing to listen to anyone who tells him exactly what he wants to here. This philosophy extends all the way to his personal doctors. While running for the presidency in 2016, Trump relied on his personal doctor, Harold Bornstein, to vouch for his good health. Bornstein would pen a letter stating that Donald Trump, "Will be the healthiest individual elected to the presidency.", which most people can tell is false just by looking at Donald Trump.

While this particular event didn't happen, early on in the COVID era Trump was looking for all types of excuses and theories to make COVID not seem as bad as it really was, so it isn't too much of a stretch that he would use something his personal doctor made up to help his cause. Despite being "the healthiest individual elected to the presidency", based on our knowledge of his eating habits he most likely doesn't consume vegetables. Blaming them for COVID is exactly the type of thing Donald Trump would do.

TS21: Fine by Easter

Date: 3/24/2020

Source:

Donald Trump made a lot of outrageous claims in his continual effort to downplay the seriousness of COVID, including making things up out of thin air. Everything was totally fine, until it wasn't. Luckily, when it wasn't totally fine, it wouldn't last long. The United States of America was going to "lockdown" for two weeks and then everything would be good to go.

Trump pushed this positive outlook on March 24, 2020 when he claimed everything would be good to go by Easter, which was just a few weeks away on April 12, 2020. In an interview with the Fox Cinematic Universe Trump said, "Wouldn't it be great to have all of the churches full? You'll have packed churches all over our country. I think it'll be a beautiful time." It turned out that everything was not "beautiful" by Easter in 2020. Things weren't even that great by Easter in 2021.

Maybe things would have turned out better if we didn't have a Mad person leading the country.

TS22: Trump Rushmore

Date: 4/14/2020
Source: FAKE NEWS

Whether this event is Real or Fake is debatable. On multiple occasions Donald Trump talked about Mount Rushmore and alluded to having his face being added with the other legendary presidents, but he never officially made the declaration to do so.

The Governor of South Dakota, Kristi Noem, used Trump's obsession with Mount Rushmore to arrange a July 4th fireworks display over the controversial monument. Surely this type of event would win Noem brownie points with Trump. She even went as far as providing Trump with a miniature model of Mount Rushmore with one addition, his face added to the monument. We eventually got a look at this model as it was seen in the background of a picture Trump took at his office in Mar-a-Lago. Trump denies claims of his dream to be added to Mount Rushmore, although it is reported a White House aide did reach out to Noem's office with a question: What's the process to add additional presidents to Mount Rushmore?

TS23: Bleach & Sunlight

Date: 4/23/2020
Source:

In a four year period filled with sheer Madness, this event easily finds a spot at the top of the list. Just a month into the COVID era Donald Trump began to become annoyed that people like Dr. Anthony Fauci, the Director of the National Institute of Allergy and Infectious Diseases, where getting attention. In Trump's Alternate Universe, no one is allowed to get more attention that Donald J. Trump. To solve this problem, Trump decided he would start giving the daily press briefings to speak directly to the American people about the COVID crisis.

During the press briefing on this date Donald Trump said, "Suppose you bring the light inside the body, which you can do through the skin, or some other way. And then I see that the disinfectant knocks it out in a minute. And is there a way we can do something like that, by injection inside." When you elect an unserious person such as Trump to be the leader of the country, in a crisis, this is what you get.

TD22: Bible Photo Op

Date: **6/1/2020**

Source:

The events that occurred during the Spring and Summer of 2020 were not kind to Donald Trump. A real leader with any sense of responsibility and sincerity may have been able to rise to the occasion. Doing so would have shown that the person was able to handle the worst of situations, rally the people of the country around a common goal, and lead the country through a difficult time. Instead, Donald Trump used law enforcement to move protestors so he could have a photo op holding a bible, upside down, at a church across near the White House.

After the murder of George Floyd by police officers, Black Lives Matter protests spread across the country. During a protest outside of the White House on May 31, 2020 a building attached to a church across the street suffered damage from a fire. The next day Trump demanded the protesters be removed from the area so he could pose with the Bible in front of the building. Trump's pathological need to always make things about himself is downright Maddening.

TD23: Trump Doesn't Do Ramps

Date: 6/13/2020

Source:

One of the few predictable things about Donald Trump is that he is always going to make fun of other people as much as possible. It is an interesting strategy to take that for some reason works for his adoring fans. Instead of bringing anything positive to the table himself, Trump simply tells you that the other people are horrible and therefore you have no other choice. You have to vote for him, otherwise you're going to have people in charge who are in physical and cognitive decline.

The even more interesting aspect of this strategy is that another predictable thing about Donald Trump is that everything he says about other people is always a projection. Trump continually accuses other people of breaking laws he constantly breaks. Additionally, he always ends up demonstrating just how physically and cognitively impaired he is himself. Before this event there has been rumors that Trump is afraid to go down steps. Little did we know, he also has a difficult time with ramps.

TW14: Killing Herman

Date: 6/20/2020

Source:

As the 2020 Presidential Election cycle started Donald Trump had a primal need to get back to what he liked best about being President, giving Maddening speeches to his adoring fans in packed venues. These "rallies" were attended by the most devout members of Trump's MAGA cult and resulted in scenes straight out of the 2006 movie Idiocracy. They are a place Donald Trump can get the only thing he truly needs, people cheering for him while he is being his Mad self. A sense of acceptance he could never receive from people with actual value to society.

Despite all advice, Trump decided to pack as many people as possible into these venues. Due to COVID protocols, the Trump Team was supposed to spread people out to allow for social distancing, but that made the crowd look smaller, which is not allowed in Trump World. Instead, they had everyone sit close together, including Herman Cain who would die of COVID a month later. Killing your supporters to fill an empty hole in your soul is utterly Maddening.

TS24: Dementia Test

Date: 7/22/2020

Source:

Despite his inability to form coherent sentences, pronounce words correctly, or make logical decisions, Donald Trump is a very stable genius. In this case, when asked by the Fox Cinematic Universe to describe his fitness for holding the office of the Presidency, Donald would detail for us a recent cognitive test he took and "aced".

"I said to the doctor — who was Dr. Ronnie Jackson — I said, is there some kind of a test? An acuity test? And he said, there actually is. And he named it, whatever it might be, and it was 30 or 35 questions. The first questions are very easy. The last questions are much more difficult, like a memory question. It's like you go, 'Person, woman, man, camera, TV.' So, they say, 'Could you repeat that?' So I said, 'Yeah. So it's person, woman, man, camera, TV.' OK. That's very good. If you get it in order, you get extra points." What are the odds "person, woman, man, camera, and TV" were the things directly in front of Trump as he told his story? Mad High.

TS25: First Pitch Dreams

Date: 7/23/2020

Source:

During the COVID era Dr. Anthony Fauci, the Director of the National Institute of Allergy and Infectious Diseases, received a lot of positive attention. Donald J. Trump quickly became jealous. Trump would sideline Dr. Fauci from speaking at White House events and even talked about firing him on a regular basis. Then Dr. Fauci was asked to throw out the first pitch at a Washington Nationals baseball game and Trump dipped into the Trump Alternate Universe, but he forgot to tell anyone else.

Up until this point in his presidency, Donald Trump had avoided throwing out the first pitch at a baseball game, which had become a tradition for Presidents. Can you imagine him throwing a pitch from a major league pitcher's mound? He'd never recover from the mocking that would surely occur. Here he claimed he was invited, and agreed, to throw out the first pitch at a New York Yankees game. Only one problem. The Yankees had no idea and this never happened. A President who just makes this up? Mad.

TW15: Rose Garden Ruiner

Date: **7/27/2020**

Source:

It wasn't an official goal of the Trumps to ruin everything they possibly could connected to the Presidency of the United States of America, but they sure did appear to try very hard to accomplish that goal. This included selecting a color scheme for the new Air Force One that matched the color scheme of his own personal Trump airplane, which he of course now calls "Trump Force One". In this plan, the current design of Air Force One that had been in use since the Kennedy Administration would be replaced, but that wouldn't be the only thing designed by the Kennedy Administration that Trump would attempt to replace.

On this date, Melania announced plans to redesign the iconic Rose Garden outside the West Wing of the White House, which was also originally designed during the Kennedy Administration. It would take a few weeks for the remodel to wrap up, but the finished product was widely panned as a major downgrade. A nice little summary of the entire Trump Presidency. Making this worse, just because he could.

TS26: Axios Interview, Uh Oh

Date: 7/28/2020

Source:

It is rare for Donald Trump to give interviews to anyone outside of the Fox Cinematic Universe. Being asked real questions and being held accountable for nonsense answers is not something Trump is capable of doing. We're not exactly sure who convinced him sitting down for this interview with Axios was a good idea, but we're pretty sure they were immediately fired. Jonathan Swan is a notoriously hard interviewer known for holding people accountable by calling them out with facts refuting their nonsense in real time. This interview was no different.

The Maddening statements Trump was corned into saying included a comment about COVID numbers, "They are dying, that's true. And you have — it is what it is. But that doesn't mean we aren't doing everything we can. It's under control as much as you can control it.", and this one about testing, "You know there are those that say you can test too much…because we've done more tests, we have more cases."

TS27: Yo-Semite

Date: 8/4/2020

Source:

Donald Trump has claimed on multiple occasions that he has "the best words" and has proved that isn't true on too many occasions to count. At one point Comedy Central's The Daily Show started putting together yearly mashups of his "Best Words" to help memorialize just how bad he is at speaking. Some of those words include:

- Diversity as Diversary
- Anonymous as Anomous
- Missiles as Mishiz
- Transplants as Transpants

In this case, while giving a speech about the United State's National Parks, Trump pronounced Yosemite (yow-seh-muh-tee) as Yo-seh-mite. Semite (seh-mite) as in anti-semite, the group of people Donald Trump has proved he is willing to accept among his followers. There have been rumors Trump can't read and either that is true or he is straight up evil. Although, both of those things are still on the table.

TS28: Rake the Forests

Date: 8/20/2020

Source:

California experienced forest fires each year Trump was president and each year Trump claimed he would withhold federal aid because they were bad at maintaining their forests, thus they were responsible for the forest fire damage. Instead, they should have listened to Trump's genius solution to solve this very complex issue. Also, withholding those funds had nothing to do with California not voting for Donald Trump to win the 2016 Presidential Election, which oddly enough seemed to be a common factor in determining whether or not Trump wanted to provide federal aid to states experiencing natural disasters.

At a rally, a place where Trump is free to be his awful self, he said, "They're starting again in California. I said, you gotta clean your floors, you gotta clean your forests — there are many, many years of leaves and broken trees and they're like, like, so flammable, you touch them and it goes up." Trump claims to have gotten this idea from Finland, but they don't know what he is talking about.

TW16: Boaters for Trump

Date: 9/5/2020
Source:

For some unknown reason, late into the 2020 Presidential Election cycle “Boaters for Trump” became a “thing”. The MAGA cult has certainly never been shy to publicly flaunt their love for Trump everywhere they can, so they fully bought into decorating their boats. As they began to congregate together to do whatever MAGA cult members do on their MAGA boats, people began to discuss the enthusiasm of Trump’s base.

These “boat parades” eventually led to people discussing how well Trump must be doing in the lead up to the election. If he can get, as Donald Trump Jr. once proclaimed was “miles and miles” of boats to gather in one spot, surely he was going to win reelection. Instead, in an even that amazingly enough did actually happen and could only actually happen in Trump World, the only thing the “Boaters for Trump” accomplished was creating a dangerous wake situation during a boat parade in Texas resulting in five of the boats sinking.

TD24: Debate Prep Covid

Date: 9/26/2020

Source:

The 2024 Republican Primary started during the course of this writing and it has been a field of mostly people who love Donald Trump, some people who are trying to pretend Donald Trump doesn't exist, and one person who seems to really not like Donald Trump anymore, former Governor of New Jersey, Chris Christie.

Donald Trump was schedule to attend the first 2020 Presidential Debate against Democratic Party Nominee Joe Biden and he turned to a former enemy turned friend turned current enemy, Chris Christie, to help him prepare. Unfortunately for Chris Christie, spending his time huddled with Donald Trump and his staff during this time period was a bad idea. A COVID outbreak would stem from multiple events held in Trump World and people involved in the debate prep were impacted, including Donald Trump and Chris Christie. While Trump would go on to the debate, with COVID, Christie would end up in the intensive care unit for seven days. No wonder why he hates Trump.

TD25: Covid? Me? No…

<u>Date:</u> 9/29/2020

<u>Source:</u>

Trump World ended up having quite the COVID outbreak during this period of time, but somehow Donald Trump had evaded the horrific virus. At least, that is what Trump World was saying. In reality, like actual reality, not Trump's Alternate Reality, Trump had tested positive for COVID three days before the first 2020 Presidential Debate. That fact Trump had COVID getting out would be damaging for his Presidential run. He was criticizing Biden as being too old, weak, and feeble to be President and now he was sick with a virus he claimed "wasn't that bad" and was "over".

Instead of telling anyone of his positive test, Trump went to the first debate. He showed up late to avoid having to be independently tested for COVID before the event, as he had agreed upon. He then went on stage and proceeded to give one of the most Maddening debate performances of all time. He put countless people at risk to help himself get reelected, because of course he did.

TS29: Stand Back & Stand By

Date: **9/29/2020**

Source:

In the midst of one of the most Maddening debate performances of all time, Donald Trump took the opportunity to help set up his plan for if he were to lose the 2020 Presidential Election. In response to a question about his thoughts on his support from white supremacist groups, Donald Trump first claimed, "I'm willing to do anything. I want to see peace. What do you want to call them? Give me a name." Joe Biden provided the Proud Boys as an example and then Donald Trump said something totally Mad, "Proud Boys, stand back and stand by."

Eventually Trump would try to clean up this statement by claiming he had no idea who the Proud Boys are, which is an incredible lie. The Proud Boys, and their extensive network connections to Trump, would listen to exactly what he told them to do. They would in fact stand back and stand by. They would be there, waiting for directions from their MAGA idol and they were willing to do whatever he needed. By the way, the Proud Boys are essentially openly Nazis.

TD26: "Working" in the Hospital

Date: **10/3/2020**

Source:

There are many Mad events connected to Donald Trump's bout with COVID in the month leading up to the 2020 Presidential Election. The situation was so unprecedented and we were dealing with one of the weird people of all time, things were bound to get Mad. Donald Trump was the sitting President of the United States of America, he was the Republican candidate for the 2020 Presidential Election, and he had contracted a virus that had decimated both the age and relative health groups he belonged to. Then they had to take Donald Trump to Walter Reed National Military Medical Center because he was having issues breathing. A Mad time indeed.

In an effort to show he was doing fine, Donald Trump did what Donald Trump usually does in situations like this. He staged a Photo Op. He couldn't continue to look weak in the minds of others, he had to do something to prove he was still able to fulfill his duties as President. Pictures of him were released showing him signing papers. The papers were blank.

TD27: Get in the Car

Date: 10/4/2020

Source:

In retrospect, when looking at Donald Trump's handling of the COVID era, one can only wonder, "Did he actively make decisions that caused people to die because he thought that was his best chance to get reelected?" Time after time, Trump was willing to put people at risk in service of himself.

Leading up to his time at Walter Reed National Military Medical Center, Trump continually put people at risk for COVID for his own gain. Thanks to him there were a ton of potential COVID spreader events within Trump World leading up to his hospitalization. The gathering for the nomination of Amy Coney Barrett to the Supreme Court of the United States. A Trump Rally in Pennsylvania. Prepping for the first debate. Then after he got bored sitting in the hospital, he made the Secret Service take him for a ride in the Presidential Limo, The Beast, so he could see the dozens of people gathered outside to support him. He made them go with him in The Beast, an airtight vehicle, while he had an airborne virus. Mad. Gross.

TD28: I… Can… Breathe… Fine

Date: 10/5/2020

Source:

On this day, Trump returned to the White House after his stay at Walter Reed National Military Medical Center to take care of his COVID symptoms. The scene Trump created upon his return looked almost as if he had planned out every single minute to make him look like a big, strong man coming back to claim his throne. Almost as if he did nothing in the hospital except for plan this event.

As the sun was beginning to set on Washington D.C., Donald Trump emerged from the hospital, totally dressed up. You know? Like how a normal person leaves a hospital. The only thing normal about the situation was him actually wearing a mask. He posed for pictures getting into the presidential limo, The Beast, and then got into Marine One to helicopter back to the White House. He got some cool looking footage as the helicopter flew across the twilight sky of D.C. and posed for pictures going back into the White House. Super cool, until he removed his mask and took the most painful looking breath of all time.

TW17: Pence's Fly

Date: **11/7/2020**

Source:

The process for selecting Donald Trump's running mate had to have looked exactly like the process for casting a season of The Celebrity Apprentice. Just a whole bunch of horrible people running as fast as possible to accept. One of those horrible people was Mike Pence. Trump determined he wasn't a threat, so he was selected to be his Vice President. Apparently Donald Trump was not the only gross creature to determine Pence wasn't a threat.

During the Vice Presidential Debate between Mike Pence and Kamala Harris a fly landed directly on Mike Pence's head. We know it landed directly on his head because the dark fly landing on Mike Pence's white hair was impossible to miss. We could all see it. The only one who didn't know was Mike Pence. Sensing Mike Pence wasn't a threat, the fly decided to hang around for a while. The 2 minute and 2 seconds the fly was on Pence's head must have felt like an entity for Donald Trump. If this was The Apprentice, Pence would definitely had been fired.

TD29: Invisible Ink Health Care Plan

Date: **10/21/2020**

Source:

From day one of his candidacy Donald Trump tried to get rid of the Affordable Care Act (ACA), which was the Obama era health care plan. Surely Trump didn't fully understand the ACA, or as it would be widely become known as, Obama Care. Trump just knew if Obama was responsible for it existing, it had to go. Donald would try multiple times during his Presidency to repeal the ACA and if it wasn't for John McCain, he might have actually done it earlier. Instead, here we are at the end of the Trump Presidency and he is still working on it.

In an attempt to garner some last minute support for the 2020 Presidential Election, Donald Trump does an interview with 60 Minutes. Like every single time Trump does an interview with someone outside of the Fox Cinematic Universe, Trump came out looking way worse. Things got so bad with this one he walked off the set early and left a Maddeningly large binder filled with his healthcare plan. It appeared to be filled with blank pages.

TW18: Four Seasons Total Landscaping

Date: 11/7/2020

Source:

Honestly, this might be the funniest thing to happen, in the history of the world. It is just a few days after the 2020 Election and there is still no official winner, despite the fact Donald Trump tried to claim victory during the night of the election. As he had convinced his cult followers to only vote in person, there was an artificial Trump lead. In a moment of pure Madness, Trump demanded they "stop the count" and name him the winner.

Due to COVID, mail-in voting was used in high volumes. They take longer to count so over the next few days, Trump World ran around saying they won, but back in reality, as expected due to Trump's own actions, the mail-in votes severely favored Joe Biden and he would eventually be named the winner. Rudy Giuliani was giving a press conference at the Four Seasons… Total Landscaping when he found out. Rudy yelled to the sky, "Everyone!?", after asking, "Says who?". The Madness began to end at a landscaping store between a crematorium and a sex shop.

TW19: Rudy is Falling Apart

Date: 11/19/2020

Source:

There a lot of people who ruined their lives in service to Donald Trump, but few have ruined them to the levels of Rudy Giuliani. After 9/11/2001, Rudy was known as America's Mayor. He tried a run or two at the Presidency and apparently went 100% Mad. This led to him latching onto Donald Trump and much like everything Donald Trump touches, Rudy Giuliani fell apart.

Rudy ended up being the one pressuring Donald Trump to claim victory the night of the 2020 Election and he would lead the charge as Trump tried to overturn the election through unfounded voter fraud claims. Currently facing a host of criminal chargers for his behavior during this time period, Rudy was involved in some serious Mad behavior. The Four Seasons Total Landscaping debacle. Farting while in court filing a frivolous lawsuit. Blowing his nose with a handkerchief and then using that handkerchief to wipe the sweat from his whole face. And yes, his hair dye melting down his face.

TS30: Get Me the Votes I Need

<u>Date:</u> 1/2/2021

<u>Source:</u>

Trump had appeared to be been spending his last few weeks in the White House figuring out how to stay. He had been spreading voter fraud conspiracy theories since the election and was attempting to use them as proof to overturn the election. As that option closed, Trump began working on contingency plans. One of those plans was to pressure states he lost into simply giving him their Electoral Votes.

We know Trump pressured multiple government officials across multiple states he lost in an effort to get them to overturn the results of the election in their state. The clearest example we have of this comes from Georgia Secretary of State, Brad Raffensperger, who recorded his phone call with Donald Trump. Trump to Raffensperger, "The people of Georgia are angry, the people in the country are angry. And there's nothing wrong with saying, you know, um, that you've recalculated. All I want to do is this. I just want to find 11,780 votes." Mad scary.

TD30: A Literal Coup

Date: **1/6/2021**

Source:

The United States Capitol Building has only ever been successfully attacked twice. The first time was during the War of 1812. The second time was on January 6, 2021. In a last ditch effort to remain in power, on the day the results of the 2020 Presidential Election were to be officially processed in the House of Representatives, Donald Trump held a rally in Washington D.C.

As he had Tweeted earlier, things did indeed get "wild". After Trump's speech, a large group of attendees marched their way to the United States Capitol Building. Seemingly at Trump's command, these marchers quickly became insurrectionists as they broke through police barricades, the police themselves, and then the doors and windows of the Capitol building. On the hunt, the mob of domestic terrorists attempted to track down members of Congress and the Vice President of the United States, Mike Pence, to delay the certification of the election.

Closing Thoughts

Well… that was depressing. There are only two ways one person could be involved in all of these events that actually happened:

1. They Are Beyond Incompetent
2. They Are Doing It On Purpose

Either way, that person should not be President of the United States of America. Or interact with society at large.

To close out Donald Trump's first impeachment, House of Representative Adam Schiff described Trump perfectly. Since he said them, his words only ring more true every single day. He prophesied, "We must say enough — enough! He has betrayed our national security, and he will do so again. He has compromised our elections, and he will do so again. You will not change him. You cannot constrain him. He is who he is. Truth matters little to him. What's right matters even less, and decency matters not at all."

After reviewing all of these events and compiling them in this fashion, I have a few more descriptions to add. Donald Trump is a man with no honor. A man without authenticity. A man who can't comprehend doing something for someone else. A man who is willing to put people in the position to die if he might get something he wants. He is wholly, completely in every possible way, unqualified to be President of the United States of America.

Ready to Vote?

The 2024 Presidential Election is right around the corner and despite facing 91 criminal indictments, Donald Trump is the current front runner, by a large margin, to be the Republican Nominee for President. He is currently facing charges for the events surrounding the Insurrection event on January 6th, 2021, committing fraud throughout his business, attempting to get officials in Georgia to commit what would have been the largest instance of voter fraud of all time, and taking, lying about taking, and trying to hide classified documents after he was President.

Luckily, it isn't that hard to keep this sorry excuse of a human from making a Volume 2 of this book necessary. The only thing you need to do is vote. Scan the QR code below to register to vote and get information on how you can vote in your area. Once you are good to vote, use this book to help others make a plan to vote and utilize it as a lifeline to anyone who is stuck in Trump's Alternate Universe.

Scan for Information About Voting

Real Events in Madness Ranking Order

Code	Madness Ranking	Event Title	Date	Page	Short URL
TD 30	10	TD30: A Literal Coup	1/6/2021	116	tinyurl.com/ylh8l58h
TD 3	9.75	TD3: Separating Children	2/2/2017	23	tinyurl.com/yqfczsux
TS 12	9.75	TS12: Cowards and Losers	11/10/2018	71	tinyurl.com/yyyvohw6
TS 30	9.75	TS30: Get Me the Votes I Need	1/2/2021	115	tinyurl.com/y7noav5x
TAW 1	9.5	TAW1: Leaked Intelligence	5/10/2017	29	tinyurl.com/yt48n9bd
TS 18	9.5	TS18: Quid Pro Quo	7/25/2019	84	tinyurl.com/yvnzvjat
TW 18	9.5	TW18: Four Seasons Total Landscaping	11/7/2020	113	tinyurl.com/y4p2chcg
TS 7	9.25	TS7: Good People Both Sides	8/15/2017	40	tinyurl.com/v7bkjh5
TAW 14	9.25	TAW14: Yes, Master Putin	7/16/2018	59	tinyurl.com/y9bmklo8
TS 29	9.25	TS29: Stand Back & Stand By	9/29/2020	106	tinyurl.com/y29xa3ks
TAW 17	9	TAW17: Rain? I'm Out.	11/10/2018	72	tinyurl.com/yak7vc47
TD 22	9	TD22: Bible Photo Op	6/1/2020	95	tinyurl.com/ycuznes3
TD 13	8.75	TD13: No Notes	7/16/2018	60	tinyurl.com/ydc2ysnz
TW 11	8.75	TW11: Fantastic Mr. Kushner	4/1/2019	78	tinyurl.com/y6oub325

Real Events in Madness Ranking Order

Code	Madness Ranking	Event Title	Date	Page	Short URL
TW 14	8.75	TW14: Killing Herman	6/20/2020	97	tinyurl.com/ygovzfgz
TD 25	8.75	TD26: Covid? Me? No...	9/29/2020	107	tinyurl.com/y2tzfg73
TD 1	8.5	TD1: Muslim Ban	1/28/2017	21	tinyurl.com/y4qffy9a
TS 23	8.5	TS23: Bleach & Sunlight	4/23/2020	94	tinyurl.com/yd9joq2w
TD 9	8.25	TD9: Paper Towels	10/3/2017	42	tinyurl.com/yuwwsq67
TS 13	8.25	TS13: Do You Still Believe?	12/24/2018	74	tinyurl.com/y8y9jaku
TS 21	8.25	TS21: Fine by Easter	3/24/2020	92	tinyurl.com/ujo3jwv
TD 8	8	TD8: Don't Look at It	8/21/2017	41	tinyurl.com/ys9r9rhc
TD 12	8	TD12: Shredding Docs	6/10/2018	55	tinyurl.com/ybhntkrk
TS 20	8	TS20: No One Can Dock	3/6/2020	90	tinyurl.com/vwlka75
TD 11	7.75	TD11: Two More Days	3/16/2018	51	tinyurl.com/yolbwpc4
TAW 11	7.75	TAW11: Saluting North Koreans	6/14/2018	56	tinyurl.com/yaq2m5oq
TAW 7	7.5	TAW7: Nuke North Korea Tweet	1/2/2018	46	tinyurl.com/yaosjf3x
TD 18	7.5	TD18: Big Member Toilet AG	11/7/2018	70	tinyurl.com/yvkzukqg

Real Events in Madness Ranking Order

Code	Madness Ranking	Event Title	Date	Page	Short URL
TD 21	7.5	TD21: Hurricane Paths	9/4/2019	87	tinyurl.com/y6eo55fw
TD 6	7.25	TD6: You're Fired	5/9/2017	28	tinyurl.com/ymmkq9wu
TS 24	7.25	TS24: Dementia Test	7/22/2020	98	tinyurl.com/y377pjor
TW 16	7.25	TW16: Boaters for Trump	9/5/2020	104	tinyurl.com/y5aqavp5
TAW 15	7	TAW15: Stand Up at the UN	9/25/2018	66	tinyurl.com/yam7pgrw
TD 28	7	TD24: I… Can… Breathe… Fine	10/5/2020	110	tinyurl.com/yum96ha3
TAW 13	6.75	TAW13: Pay Me to Protect Me	7/14/2018	58	tinyurl.com/vxyo4mc
TW 12	6.75	TW12: Ivanka, Serious Politician	6/29/2019	82	tinyurl.com/y2ol2cl7
TS 26	6.75	TS26: Axios Interview, Uh Oh	7/28/2020	101	tinyurl.com/ynngdgv7
TD 27	6.75	TD28: Get in the Car	10/4/2020	109	tinyurl.com/yqxce39y
TAW 16	6.5	TAW16: Trump Hearts Un	9/29/2018	67	tinyurl.com/ybpomjgc
TAW 21	6.5	TAW21: ISIS Leader, Died Like a Dog	10/26/2019	89	tinyurl.com/y47xys67
TS 6	6.25	TS6: Boy Scouts & Sex Parties	7/24/2017	38	tinyurl.com/ysgmleo4
TS 8	6.25	TS8: Invisible F-35s	11/23/2017	45	tinyurl.com/yd2bgjes

Real Events in Madness Ranking Order

Code	Madness Ranking	Event Title	Date	Page	Short URL
TS 28	6.25	TS28: Sweep the Forests	8/20/2020	103	tinyurl.com/yxkt2ghs
TS 1	6	TS1: CIA Crowd Size	1/21/2017	17	tinyurl.com/gs6bt2r
TS 19	6	TS19: Nuke Hurricanes	8/25/2019	86	tinyurl.com/252z8bnr
TAW 4	5.75	TAW4: Trump in Front	5/25/2017	34	tinyurl.com/yuus4hqq
TAW 10	5.75	TAW10: World Leader Scold	6/9/2018	54	tinyurl.com/y2wx9lbp
TS 17	5.75	TS17: Revolutionary War Planes	7/4/2019	83	tinyurl.com/yyokkezo
TD 29	5.75	TD29: Invisible Ink Health Care Plan	10/21/2020	112	tinyurl.com/yttzcfqx
TS 3	5.5	TS3: Civil Civil War	5/1/2017	26	tinyurl.com/yrgmauuq
TW 7	5.25	TW7: Drunk Doctor	1/16/2018	48	tinyurl.com/yeet9egk
TS 5	5	TS5: Covfefe	5/31/2017	35	tinyurl.com/y75cyvat
TW 2	4.5	TW2: Alternative Facts	1/22/2017	19	tinyurl.com/y6wqmkch
TS 15	4.5	TS15: Windmill Cancer	4/2/2019	79	tinyurl.com/2krg89bf
TS 4	4.25	TS4: Steam Powered Navy	5/11/2017	30	tinyurl.com/ycj8o794
TAW 5	4.25	TAW5: Local Milk People	8/3/2017	39	tinyurl.com/ymfpemq5

Real Events in Madness Ranking Order

Code	Madness Ranking	Event Title	Date	Page	Short URL
TAW 6	4.25	TAW6: Japanese Fish Food	11/6/2017	43	tinyurl.com/ywlsmmr9
TW 8	4.25	TW8: Drunk Nunberg	3/5/2018	49	tinyurl.com/ymdknedo
TS 10	4.25	TS10: Wet Hurricanes	9/18/2018	65	tinyurl.com/y75rxn58
TD 19	4.25	TD19: Fast Food Champs	1/14/2019	75	tinyurl.com/ycumd3wh
TD 24	4.25	TD25: Debate Prep Covid	9/26/2020	105	tinyurl.com/2x7ax924
TW 1	4	TW1: Sean Spicer	1/21/2017	18	tinyurl.com/yadm5asv
TW 19	4	TW19: Rudy is Falling Apart	11/19/2020	114	tinyurl.com/yxsyuboq
TD 5	3.75	TD5: Two Scoops	5/8/2017	27	tinyurl.com/y74q8stt
TW 5	3.75	TW5: The Scaramucci Era	7/21/2017	37	tinyurl.com/yrfctcnb
TS 27	3.75	TS27: Yo-Semite	8/4/2020	102	tinyurl.com/y3qovkfp
TD 10	3.5	TD10: Can't Drink Water	11/15/2017	44	tinyurl.com/y9l877wn
TAW 12	3.5	TAW12: Where is the Queen?	7/13/2018	57	tinyurl.com/y94cvyj7
TD 20	3.5	TD20: Get McCain Out of Here	5/28/2019	80	tinyurl.com/yyx8elr2
TD 16	3.25	TD16: Big Men Always Crying	9/7/2018	64	tinyurl.com/ymhyt8xk

Real Events in Madness Ranking Order

Code	Madness Ranking	Event Title	Date	Page	Short URL
TW 10	3	TW10: Creepy Christmas	11/26/2018	73	tinyurl.com/yckoro6a
TS 14	3	TS14: Tim Apple, CEO of Cook	3/6/2019	76	tinyurl.com/y57zteau
TD 23	3	TD23: Trump Doesn't Do Ramps	6/13/2020	96	tinyurl.com/ylmkfq6j
TD 26	3	TD27: "Working" in the Hospital	10/3/2020	108	tinyurl.com/yyefbrdn
TD 4	2.75	TD4: Trump Loves Trucks	3/23/2017	25	tinyurl.com/ypqh2g29
TD 17	2.75	TD17: Kanye in the Oval	10/11/2018	69	tinyurl.com/yccq5gkx
TAW 2	2.5	TAW2: The Orb	5/21/2017	32	tinyurl.com/k4k687u
TW 4	2.5	TW4: The Wedding Planner	6/16/2017	36	tinyurl.com/ymbu4y3q
TS 25	2.5	TS25: First Pitch Dreams	7/23/2020	99	tinyurl.com/y5wwkxg7
TW 9	2.25	TW9: Trump, Cohen, Hannity	4/16/2018	52	tinyurl.com/yobgk6kw
TAW 19	2.25	TAW19: Buying Greenland	8/18/2019	85	tinyurl.com/y2g6ucg7
TW 17	2	TW17: Pence's Fly	10/7/2020	111	tinyurl.com/yu3do2wp
TW 6	1.75	TW6: The Wolff of White House	1/5/2018	47	tinyurl.com/ykg5vh8w
TS 9	1.75	TS9: Need ID?	7/31/2018	61	tinyurl.com/yprqhy9o

Real Events in Madness Ranking Order

Code	Madness Ranking	Event Title	Date	Page	Short URL
TW 15	1.75	TW15: Rose Garden Ruiner	7/27/2020	100	tinyurl.com/y6jpkc7n
TAW 3	1.5	TAW3: Trump Meets Pope	5/24/2017	33	tinyurl.com/yqzqomgt
TAW 8	1.5	TAW8: Trump No More	3/5/2018	50	tinyurl.com/ytwwz9ct
TS 16	1.25	TS16: The Moon & Mars	6/7/2019	81	tinyurl.com/yxfx25zy

Trump Madness Bracket

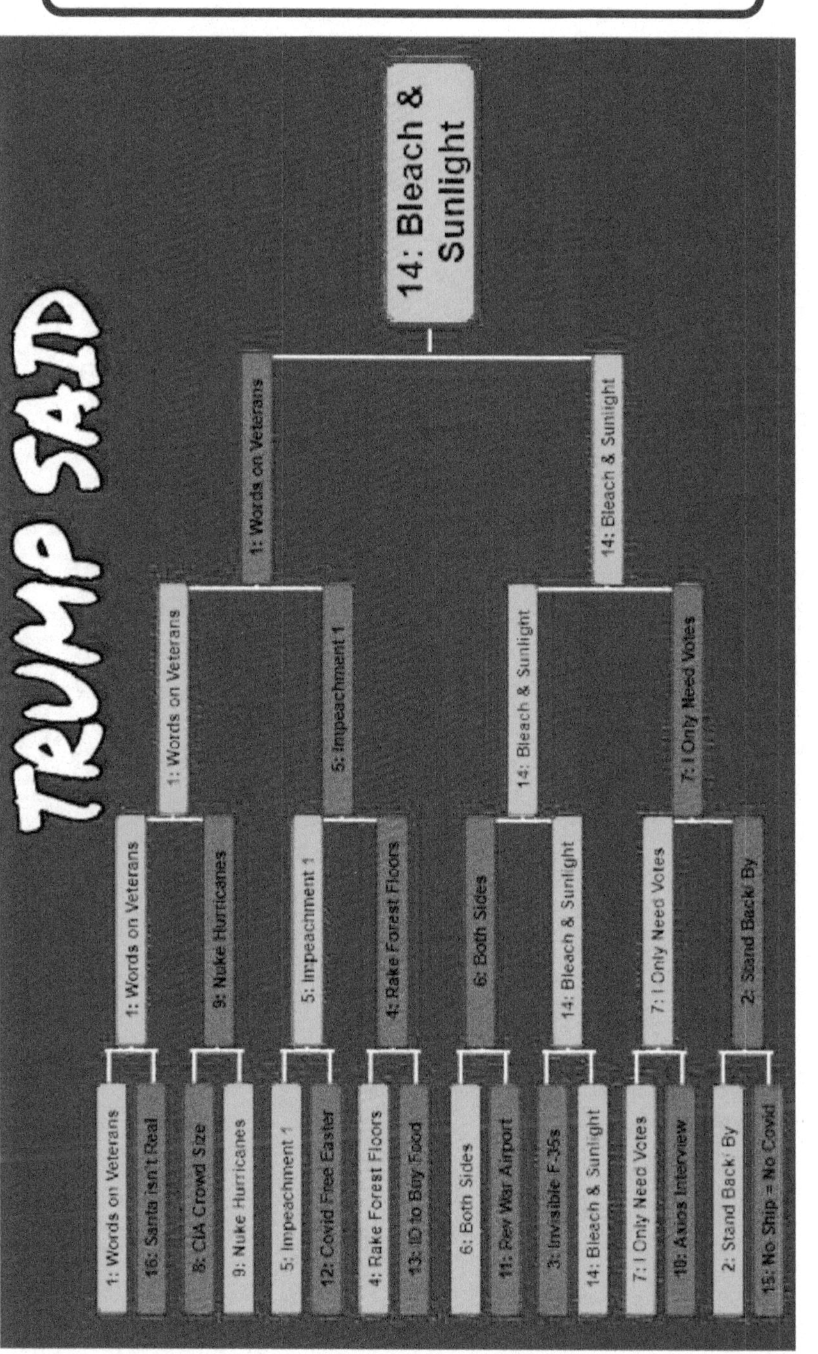

Trump Madness Bracket

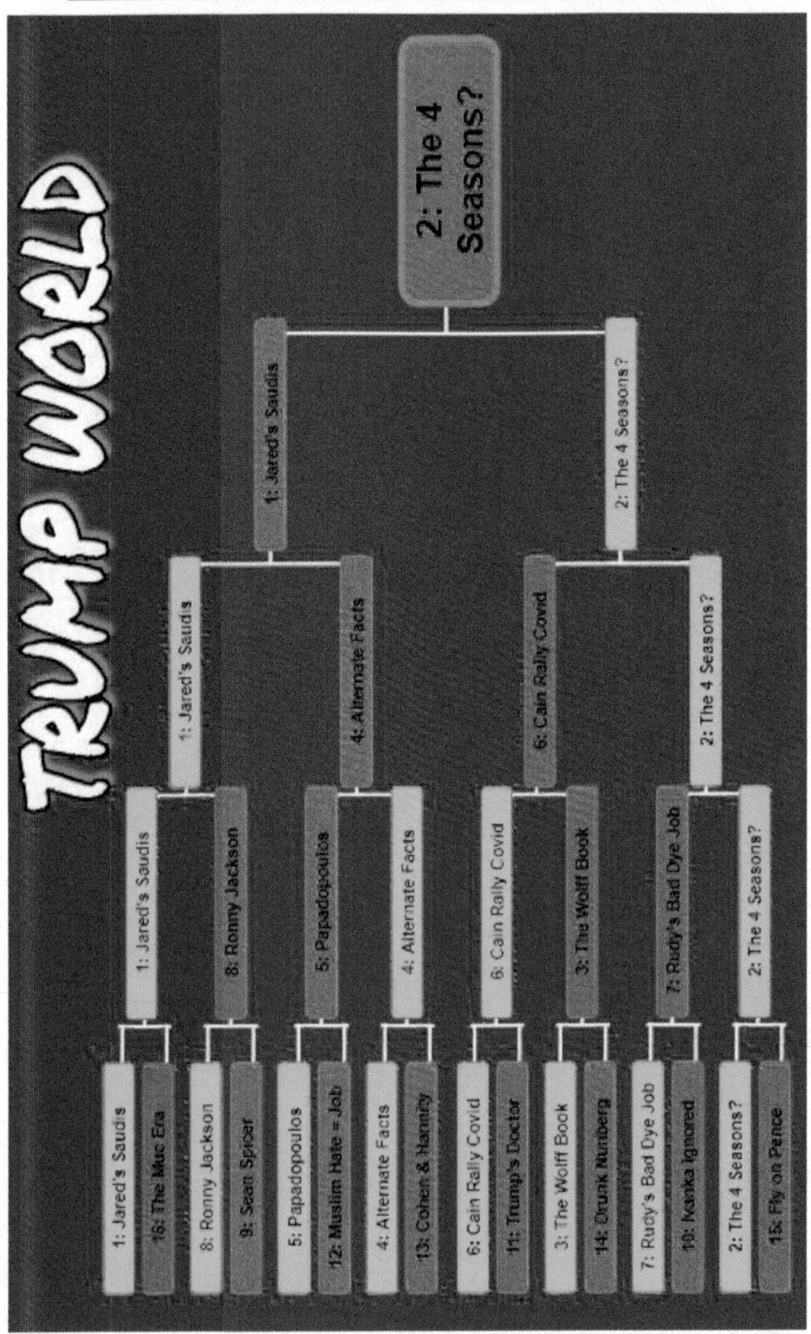

Trump Madness Bracket

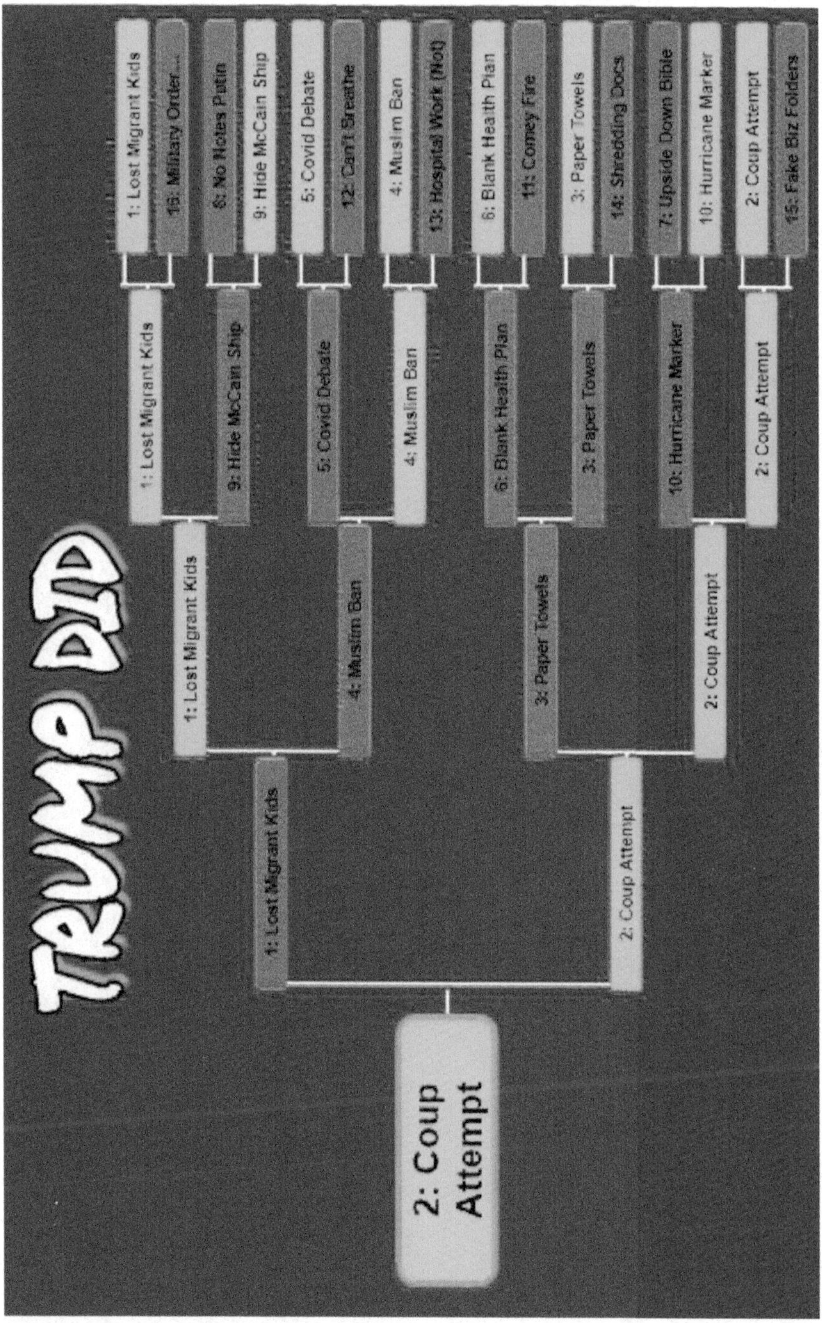

TRUMP DID

1: Lost Migrant Kids
16: Military Order...
8: No Notes Putin
9: Hide McCain Ship
5: Covid Debate
12: Can't Breathe
4: Muslim Ban
13: Hospital Work (Not)
6: Blank Health Plan
11: Comey Fire
3: Paper Towels
14: Shredding Docs
7: Upside Down Bible
10: Hurricane Marker
2: Coup Attempt
15: Fake Biz Folders

1: Lost Migrant Kids
9: Hide McCain Ship
5: Covid Debate
4: Muslim Ban
6: Blank Health Plan
3: Paper Towels
10: Hurricane Marker
2: Coup Attempt

1: Lost Migrant Kids
4: Muslim Ban
3: Paper Towels
2: Coup Attempt

1: Lost Migrant Kids
2: Coup Attempt

2: Coup Attempt

Trump Madness Bracket

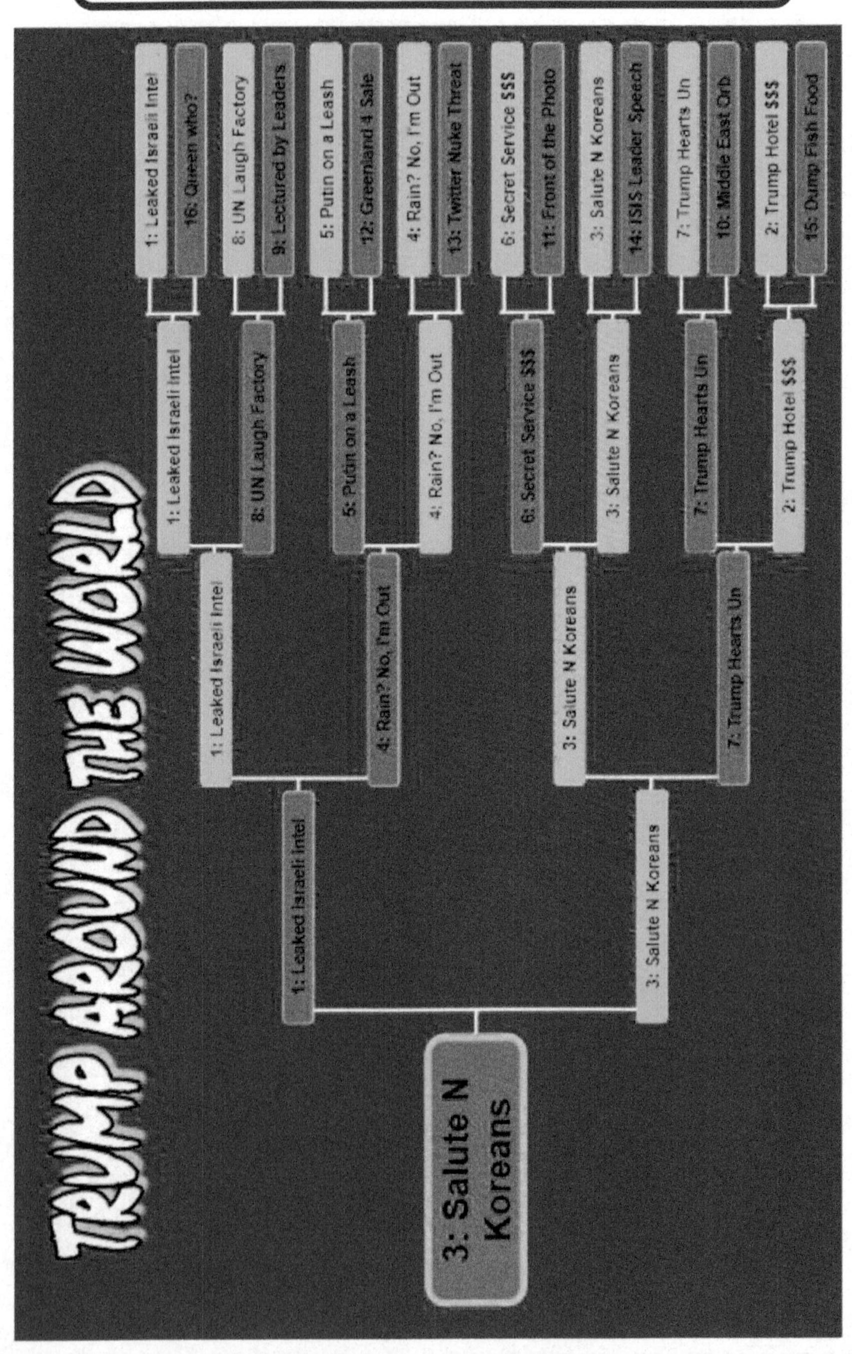

Trump Madness Bracket

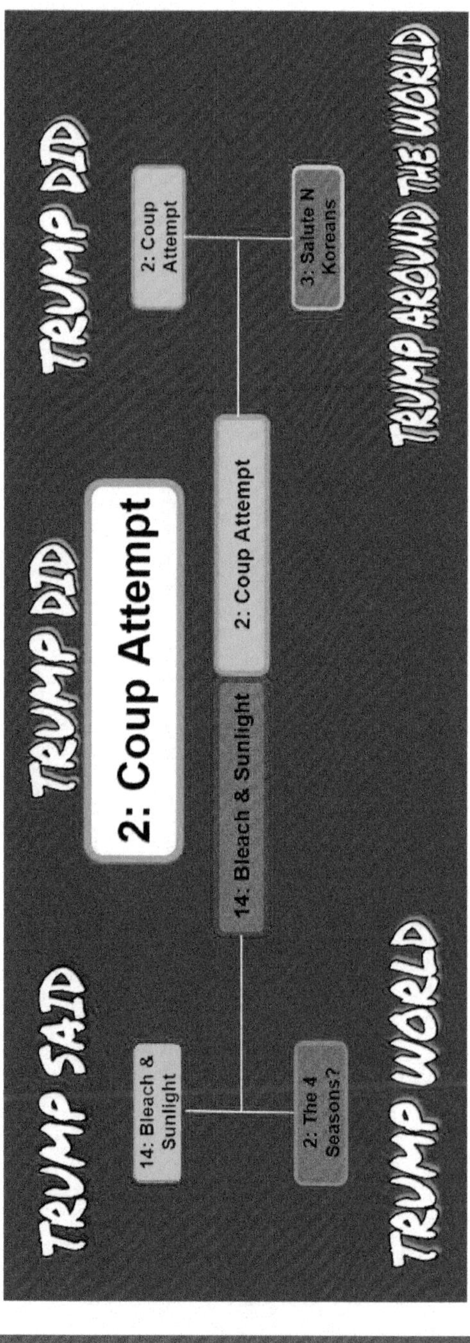

Printed in Great Britain
by Amazon